PICKER'S
POCKET·GUIDE

SIGNS

How to Pick Antiques like a Pro

ERIC BRADLEY

Published by

Krause Publications, a division of F+W, A Content + eCommerce Company
700 East State Street • Iola, WI 54990-0001
715-445-2214 • 888-457-2873
www.krausebooks.com

To order books or other products call toll-free 1-800-258-0929
or visit us online at www.krausebooks.com

More information about the signs pictured on the cover can be found on the following pages: Top row, from left: P. 132, P. 99, P. 24; **bottom row, from left**: P. 8, P. 110, P. 148, P. 81. **Back cover, top row from lef**t: P. 156, P. 48, P. 114 and P. 106; **bottom row, from left**: P. 53, P. 177, and P. 175.

ISBN-13: 978-1-4402-4217-5
ISBN-10: 1-4402-4217-8

Designed by: Jana Tappa
Edited by: Kristine Manty

Printed in China

Foreword

In a time when many are looking for the "next big thing," some of us are still looking for the last one. That is why, after 35 years of buying, selling, and collecting antique advertising, it is so exciting to see a younger person picking up the gauntlet of enthusiasm started by those who documented this hobby early on such as Jim Cope and Ray Klug. Eric Bradley is just that person. I have followed his career as a writer in the antiques industry and his genuine love and passion for antiques in general shows through in everything he does. I was very pleased when he stopped by my office and told me about this book. He asked for my opinion on his ideas, so I shared with him a few stories of pieces found, some lost and some I had sold. As we were talking, the gleam in his eye told me he had been bitten by the same bug that has drawn many of us to collecting signage. Perhaps Eric is just the right person to bring antique sign collecting into the next century and help to attract new collectors.

With its brief tutorial on the history of advertising and explanation of terms, this book gives the budding collector an excellent place to start. The images encourage the collector to find his or her own niche categories, whether they are early lithographic art or 1960s pop art. Eric walks the reader through many different types of advertising that can have a general appeal, such as gas and oil, soda pop, and household advertising. But he also pictures some distinct rarities heavily sought after within the hobby.

When I served as a board member for the Antique Advertising Association, I realized how important sharing and educating new collectors was to the longevity of our hobby. This book is not meant to be a literal message about the value of specific signs but it is meant to be used as a tool to encourage future sign collectors to fall in love with collecting. I think even a seasoned collector will appreciate the spirit and enthusiasm this book conveys.

— *Marsha Dixie*
Dallas, Texas
April 9, 2014

Introduction

A good sign catches your eye: A shock of orange. A flash of Spencerian script. A friendly face that was as familiar in your grandma's kitchen as she was.

The reasons we are drawn to vintage advertising signs today is partly due to the effectiveness of the signs in the first place. They are designed to catch our attention. But their appeal to collectors and pickers is much deeper than the original ad message. Maybe the sign reminds them of five-cent Coke floats after school or an afternoon of fishing. Maybe it's the true artistry behind the work itself: the subject, the shape, the font, the colors, lines, and its historical significance.

All of these factors came together the instant I spotted a unique counter-top sign. Shortly after relocating to the Dallas-Fort Worth area to work at Heritage Auctions, the world's largest collectibles auctioneer, I was browsing one of the many innovative collectibles shops downtown. A sign caught my attention right away. The dealer set it high in the booth and it was surrounded by smalls, which made it stand out even more. The plywood sign was cut in the shape of the state of Wisconsin and hand-painted with the words, "Slack's Wisconsin's Finest Jams and Jellies."

Having just moved from The Dairy State, the sign's shape had me hooked immediately. It reminded me of the familiar jigsaw-cut signs in use during the 1930s-1950s, the heyday of upper Midwest tourism. The fonts and four-color style gave me a hint it probably dated to the 1960s. The condition of the board and fact the paint wasn't faded told me someone took care of it, which meant it was probably not used outside and had been

The visual appeal, the memories, and history all come together in advertising and the passion for these functional works of art is growing.

shielded by the harmful effects of direct sunlight. All of these factors culminated in the nostalgic message: A wholesome product made by a humble operation in God's country.

I could barely wait to learn why this company called Slack's would have gone through the trouble to create this sign by hand. A quick internet search later, I was delighted to learn Slack's was still in business and still making jams and jellies. Back in the summer of 1954, a farm wife named Viola Slack made some jam from the wild blackberries that grew along dusty gravel roads in South Central Wisconsin. She and her husband Earl sold the jam door to door and to tourists. The jam became popular and soon their whole family was making several varieties for small area grocery stores. The company

Trade sign for Slack's Jams & Jellies, 18-1/5" h x 16" w, found at DFW M'Antiques in Dallas. The sign was hand-painted in the 1960s by members of the Slack family, who are still selling their spreads and salsas at small grocery stores in Wisconsin and online at slacksjellyfarm.com.

Eric Bradley

now has eight employees and a busy mail-order business on-line, in addition to a strong retail business. It even runs a small antiques shop attached to a retail store north of Madison, Wis.

I sent photos of the sign to the staff at Slack's to let them know it still exists and to learn more about when it might have been made. Jacki Slack, who manages the shipping side of the business, was thrilled to learn about the discovery. She said the sign dates from the 1960s or the early 1970s. "That's the time period when we had the Wisconsin-shaped gold labels," she said. "Either my uncle or my brother made the sign. It's probably the only one made to use for the display in a lean-to on the side of the barn that we used to sell out of years ago!"

Signs like this are in demand because they blend visual appeal, memories, and history in one visually-appealing display. Passion for these functional works of art are growing.

Thanks in part to HISTORY's *American Pickers* and a host of reality television shows, a whole new generation of Americans is looking at advertising signs in a new light. A December 2013 advertising auction saw more than 50 auction records across tobacciana, Coca-Cola, and soda pop advertising categories. A 100-lot single-owner collection of items advertising Whistle soda, described as "one of the largest known collections of its type," held a rare, circa-1930s tri-fold cardboard cutout featuring two boys wooing a girl – one with roses, the other with a more-enticing bottle of Whistle. Measuring 31 inches x 36 inches, the sign sold to an internet bidder for $38,400 against an estimate of $1,500-$2,500.

"One of the things I've found is that advertising signs cross all demographics – young, old, male, female," said Dan Morphy, President of Morphy Auctions. "Collectors view them as art. Instead of buying a painting for their wall, a collector will display a piece of advertising. Many people who collect antique advertising signs are advertising or marketing professionals,

This rare, circa-1930s tri-fold cardboard cutout advertising sign for Whistle Soda fetched $38,400 at auction in late 2013 at Morphy Auctions.

so they appreciate the art and presentation. A lot of younger people who are collecting also come from the advertising and marketing world."

Morphy said the price of the tri-fold Whistle soda sign is a textbook example when two collectors battle to own a scarce piece of advertising. Whistle Orange Soda was introduced in 1925 and primarily distributed around the St. Louis, Mo., area. That puts the tri-fold sign early in the product's life and likely limited the distribution to an area near the factory. When you consider the piece is a store display not intended for private ownership, it's dramatic, colorful and funny graphics, and its excellent condition given its composition, it's easier to see why it set a five-figure auction record. The advertising sign's auction price is in the ballpark of an original work by artist Marc Chagall, which just goes to show the status advertising signs have with collectors.

IN THIS BOOK

This guide will show you where to find the good, better, and best advertising signs to pick or keep for your own collection – no matter what your collecting level – as well as show you

Mr. Peanut debuted after 1916 following a nation-wide contest to develop a new mascot for Planter's Peanuts. The character's enduring charm, as first illustrated in this magazine advertisement, is the subject of a new ad campaign that kicked off in 2012.

how to sell your signs for the best money possible. Availability, condition, composition, message, and age all play a factor in an advertising sign's collectability and value. All of these factors can be

highly nuanced and this book aims to show you how to understand what collectors look for. It will also touch on the history of advertising, look at common fakes and reproductions, and give you a working vocabulary to speak and think intelligently about this exciting and varied field.

As you read the book, pay special attention to the "Picker's Tip" boxes distributed across its chapters. These tips, factoids, and tactics will help you in the field. For instance, did you know that the dapper Mr. Peanut character made famous in Planter's Peanuts ads was not created by a Madison Avenue marketing executive, but by a 13-year-old girl in 1916? The appearance of Mr. Peanut on advertising signs can help you determine the date it was created if you find it in a shop or show or at a country auction.

The world of advertising signs stretches as far as the imagination, so for the sake of brevity and relevance, we will review the most popular collecting areas that see the most demand and represent some of the most beautiful signs known to exist. Feel free to use what you learn here and apply it to an area or subset that interests you the most.

Some people collect signs featuring Santa Claus, while others focus on a particular brand or, broader still, a particular product. A collection of coffee advertising is striking, as is a collection of signs and material devoted to Hires Root Beer. There are no rules on what to collect but there are criteria all valuable collections have in common: Condition, Authenticity, Provenance, Exposure, and Quality. We will illustrate these criteria through the best examples in their respective fields. I once read an article on how food critics hone their ability to judge food. "Try the best and judge the rest" is the message I

Advertising signs are considered the "everyman's art." They were produced from a variety of materials and sizes, making them common finds at antiques and collectibles shows. Spanning food, roadside signs, automobilia, Coca-Cola, and even a bakery trade sign, this display by dealers Don and Marta Orwig shows the depth and breadth of signs available to collectors and pickers.

Brian Maloney

took away from their methods. By looking at examples of Good, Better, Best, you'll begin to develop an eye for quality advertising and what makes it so.

We'll also touch base with some of the most effective and accomplished collectors and sellers in the field. Thousands of pickers base their livelihood on finding unique advertising signs and reselling them to collectors or businesses. Their skill and techniques were perfected over decades of trial and error, but they are happy to share their knowledge about the market and why they do what they do.

I hope all of this inspires you to get out and about, make new friendships, and start a fresh hunt for some of the most beautiful collectibles ever made.

Signs in high demand feature similar design elements and collectors are drawn to originality. Generally speaking, signs are composed of five main elements or parts: a headline, a sub-headline or tagline, product benefits, an image, or a call to action.

Company name

Product name

Product benefits

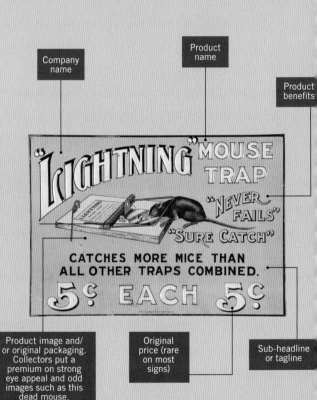

Product image and/ or original packaging. Collectors put a premium on strong eye appeal and odd images such as this dead mouse.

Original price (rare on most signs)

Sub-headline or tagline

Lightning Mouse Trap sign, circa 1900, rare embossed tin litho sign by The H.D. Beach Co., Coshocton, Ohio, retains original cardboard backing and string hangar, very good to excellent, 9-1/2" x 6-1/2", **$3,900**.

Morphy Auctions

CHAPTER 1

Explaining Advertising Signs

Although countless shapes and methods of advertising mediums exist, the advertising sign is generally defined as having words or pictures that give information about a product or service. Signs are a valuable and powerful tool for commerce. Prior to the Industrial Revolution (1760 to 1850) most signs were carved in wood, engraved in stone or directly into walls. Trade signs were carved by hand and hung outside the businesses themselves.

As technology increased and printing became commercialized, posters, bills, billboards, and other forerunners of the modern sign were attached to boards.

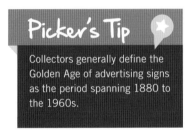

Picker's Tip

Collectors generally define the Golden Age of advertising signs as the period spanning 1880 to the 1960s.

The first newspaper advertisements to appear in the United States – an offer for a reward for the return of two stolen anvils - were printed in the *Boston News-Letter* in April 1704.[1] The first newspaper ads to appear in England – two ads with line drawings for shipping companies - did not appear until Jan. 1, 1788 in London's *The Times* newspaper.[2]

It wasn't until a consumer-driven society emerged during the mid-1800s that advertising signs became a valuable and affordable pursuit for businesses. By 1848, posters were commonplace and became more aesthetically pleasing after the development of lithography. During the 1860s, a German refugee named Louis Prang perfected a method to introduce

1 *America for Sale.*
2 *Twentieth Century Advertising.*

literally dozens of colors into the printing process by creating drawings on stone. For his work on book illustrations, Prang sometimes used more than 30 stones, each devoted to a separate color for a printing process he called "chromo-lithography." Collector and author Jay T. Last, in his wonderful book exploring the development of 19th century American lithography, *The Color Explosion: Nineteenth-Century American Lithography*, states the basic concepts used in original lithographic processes in the late 19th century are responsible for the wonderful signs we collect. The process has not changed in principle for more than 200 years.

The U.S. Civil War was a chief turning point in American life and marked a distinct shift from rural life to an urbanization of the country. The addition of color printing opened demand for more intricate images and led to a boon time for commercial artists. Sign development exploded at this time and the late 1860s through the 1870s mark the real beginning of the advertising sign as we know it. Preserving images, slogans, and directions on a more permanent material made economic sense over the long run.

Massive investment in England, Europe, and America to create printing machines, enameling processes, printing on tin, and distribution methods made advertising signs a smart move to reach more customers. Two newspaper publishers in particular remained at the cutting edge of sign production during the late 19th century on the banks of Ohio's Muskinum River.

AMERICAN ART WORKS & STANDARD ADVERTISING CO., COSHOCTON, OHIO

Thanks to a winner-take-all feud between two newspaper publishers, collectors today are treated to wonderfully detailed tin advertising signs produced in Coshocton, Ohio. Publisher Jasper Freemont Meek spun off his booming advertising business to create the Tuscarora Advertising Co. (1887-1901) and is credited for the concept behind the annual advertising calendar. Meeks was one of the first sign makers in the world to adopt offset lithography in 1895. He used the technology from the stone plates to print images on a rubber blanket in order to print tin signs.

Across town, publisher Henry Beach founded the Stan-

Rare American Art Works Company Stoneware tin sign, by The American Art Works Company of Coshocton, Ohio, reads "STONEWARE/THE BEST FOOD/CONTAINER" at the top and "WE SELL ALL SIZES" on the bottom, cardboard with a folding stand, back is stamped with The American Art Works cleaning instructions, 19" x by 13". **$600**.

Rock Island Auction Co.

dard Advertising Co. (1888-1901) to compete in lockstep with Meeks. Initially, Beach sought to brand anything he could get to fit under a printing press and is credited with inventing the advertising yard stick. Standard Advertising is the company that produced the rare – and highly controversial – Campbell's Soup American flag sign (see Chapter 3, P. 43).

The two rivals merged in 1901 as the "Meek and Beach Co." but they couldn't agree on much of anything and Meeks bought out Beach's share and renamed the company Meek Company (1905-1909). When Meek retired, the company was renamed American Art Works (1909-1950). The company was responsible for fantastic cardboard and tin signs advertising fishing tackle for Horton Mfg. Co., Kellogg's Toasted Corn Flakes, and Coca-Cola.

Beach moved a New York printing business to Coshocton, which he renamed the H.D. Beach Co. in 1901. Specializing in signs, his firm produced advertising for De Laval Cream Separators, Pennsylvania Bicycle Tires, Miller's Brewing, and Budweiser.

If the printers of the 18th and 19th centuries gave us the technology to print signs, it was the 20th century's Mad Men who perfected the delivery and the message. Agencies such as Lord & Thomas in Chicago, J. Walter Thompson in New York and S.H. Benson in London employed a stable of artists and copywriters for targeted ad campaigns and engaged in market research to perfect slogans and images.[3] The only thing stopping a company from producing a line of permanent, colorful, advertisements was the amount of money they were willing to spend on the effort.

"When it comes to the actual subject matter used on these signs," says Dan Morphy, President of Morphy Auctions, "the artists designing and illustrating them obviously considered eye appeal, subject matter, and color. This tells us they were paying attention to the general audience of consumers who would be buying the product."

The power advertising wields on our daily life cannot be understated. And as we'll see, companies used this power to the maximum advantage to change how America made its purchasing decisions and even influence its collective popular culture. Signs that were most effective in this dual pursuit remain the most popular with collectors.

---

3 *Twentieth Century Advertising.*

Punch & Judy Cocktail celluloid sign, captioned "Drink a Punch & Judy Cocktail – It Recuperates" with a cardboard easel, has a colorful cameo inset of Punch & Judy, The Punch & Judy Co., Maywood, NJ. Reverse label reads "Crystaloid" sign made by Whitehead & Hoag Co. Newark, NJ, retains original brown paper factory wrapping and is New Old Stock in near excellent condition, appears to never have been used, rare, 12" w x 7" h, **$1,761.75**.

James D. Julia, Inc.

WHAT SIGNS ARE MADE OF

Substrate materials used to create signs are limited to the most cost effective materials available at the time, but generally are limited to glass, vitrolite, paper, fiberglass, aluminum, cardboard, tin, steel, and wood. The images themselves might be held fast with painted on, transfer printing, celluloid, plastic or through a process called decalcomania.

The additions of frames gave signs a sense of permanence, which encouraged business owners to keep them around a bit longer than usual. Frames also help to preserve ads painted or printed on more delicate mediums such as paper, glass and cardboard. Saving a few pennies, many designers of tin and steel advertising signs incorporated a frame motif printed along with the actual image and these creations are now referred to as self-framed signs.

As with all art, the ability for the artist and the printer to bring these disparate elements together drives home the collectability and value of a sign. Collectors are generally drawn to detailed signs, but that's not always the case. Collectors of

In this photo taken in July of 1938, the fence behind a grocery store in Baltimore, Md., is literally plastered with advertising signs and shows how prevalent outdoor advertising was in urban areas.

simple Whistle Soda advertising from the 1930s may be just as thrilled to own a large litho sign as much as the collector of a Union Mills Flour ads is to own an intricate portrait of a Native American warrior surrounded by detailed scenes of the Wild West and frontier life.

As different as they may be, both of these signs share the same five basic elements. The more elements represented in an

ad, the more likely it is to appeal to more collectors, which in turn affects values. This is especially the case if the sign features celebrities or references to historical influences, or is a brand that has become a household name. One major caveat to this rule is Coca-Cola signs, which turned the retail world on its head by elevating the advertising sign into a unique American art form.

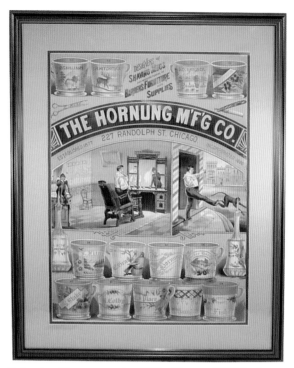

Barber shop litho on paper, circa 1870s, "Hornung M'F'G' Co.," Chicago, litho with amusing barbershop graphics, professionally framed, near mint, 22" h x 16" w, **$2,200**.

Rich Penn Auctions

Offset printed advertisement for the "American Lithographic Company New York," 1919, featuring painting of a Native American making a headdress or war bonnet by artist E. I. Couse, 18" w x 9-3/4" h, housed in a 22" w x 13-1/2" h frame, **$625**.

Heritage Auctions

A No. 1 Chocolate Brownies, circa 1880s, single-sided lithograph on tin cardboard, detail includes a possible Palmer Cox-style Brownies carrying a stack of chocolate candies, very good, 6" square, **$300-$400**.

Heritage Auctions

Spitting prohibited porcelain enamel sign, 8" x 4-1/4", part of a set that sold for **$488**.

Rock Island Auction Co.

A rather famous photo of a country store on a dirt road shows how vintage advertising signs were originally displayed by stores. Interestingly, the only signs hanging outside advertise soda pop and cigarettes, the two industries that engaged in the most aggressive ad campaigns in American history. This rather famous photo was taken on a Sunday afternoon in Gordonton, N.C., in July 1939 by Dorthea Lang for the Farm Security Administration.

Photo courtesy Library of Congress Prints and Photographs/
Office of War Information Black-and-White Negatives

This rare 1954 Joe Lowe Company paper sign features Abbott and Costello in an ad for Popsicle frozen treats, excellent, 11" x 15", **$191**.

Heritage Auctions

CHAPTER 2

Product Branding

Advertising has been called the every man's art.

"It really was the closest people came in those days to real art," said Wayne Yoder, owner of W. Yoder Auctions, a Wisconsin auctioneer who has watched collector's tastes evolve from furniture to high-end signs. "They were everywhere at the time and they had true art that people still want to own today."

To understand the passion behind collecting advertising it helps to understand the art and the ad campaigns that created them. Both were not created by chance. Signs are the end result of market study, product study, consumer sentiment, and return on investment. Graphics are punchy, beautiful, visually arresting, and designed to capture your attention in a tenth of a second. Even the plainest signs collected today have some aspect of graphic design that catches a collector's eye, even if the value isn't terribly high.

Signs are the wellspring of a consumer-driven economy. A robust middle class America was the chief driver of this advertising boom. As such, most ads are for consumer products marketed to this consumption class, such as gasoline, soft drinks, beer, alcohol, food stuffs, and various other consumables. Consumables like these required a steady stream of advertising to maintain sales against competitors. These remain the most popular and most valuable signs among collectors.

Signs made to promote goods that are not customarily produced or distributed for sale to consumers are also sought after by collectors, but on the whole they generally do not enjoy the same level of collectability as signs promoting non-consumer goods. For instance, a 27-inch sign for Armour's Animal and Poultry Feeds, which was marketed exclusively to livestock farmers, may currently be found at auction for roughly $800. A 27-inch sign advertising Coca-Cola may be had for roughly $1,900. Both signs may have avid collecting bases but Coke

Armour's Feeds tin sign, 27", **$825**.
W. Yoder Auctions

enjoys more household brand awareness than Armour's animal feeds, despite its catchy tagline promising greater profits.

The advertising sign boon between the years of 1880 and 1960 was influenced by three important developments:

- Characters, some of whom are still in use today
- Fonts as design
- American artists who successfully transitioned from commercial art to fine art

ADVERTISING CHARACTERS — THEN AND NOW

During the last 150 years, marketers have invented thousands of advertising mascots, trademarks, characters, and personas to capture consumer's attention. Bibendum, commonly referred to as the Michelin Man, and RCA's Nipper the dog, both first appearing in the 1890s, Cracker Jack's Sailor Jack and his dog Bingo and Wrigley Gum's Sprightly Spearmen, appearing in the 1910s, Reddy Kilowatt in the 1920s, and Willie the Penguin for Kool Cigarettes appearing in the 1930s, are just a few of the thousands of characters created to appear in advertisements, especially signs.

The pace picked up in the Post–World War II baby boom between the years 1946 and 1964. This period marked the first time advertising was specifically targeted toward children. An added bonus, it cost less in the long run to create a character than pay royalties to a celebrity. Another affordable work-around was using someone else's popular character on your sign and there was no shortage of these in American newspaper comic strips.

COMIC STRIP CHARACTERS ON SIGNS

Comic strip characters were often used on signs. Cartoonist Palmer Cox is credited as the first to use his band of chubby characters he called "The Brownies" in the first of its kind, mass-market advertising push during the late 19th century and early 20th century. The characters were used to sell everything from books, dishes, drinks, and even whiskey. Kodak used the cartoony sprites to market its best-selling "Brownie Camera." A Brownie drink cardboard advertisement sign with a metal frame made by the M.C.A. Sign Co. and measuring 21 inches wide by 60 inches high sold for $400 in January 2014 at a Victorian Casino Antiques auction. It's been said Walt Disney himself based his marketing plan for Mickey Mouse on Cox's Brownies.

The Brownies and American comic strip writer and artist Richard F. Outcault's character Buster Brown and The Yellow Kid were among the first to appear on American advertising signs in the early 1900s. Few creators held back. Little Orphan Annie appears on signs for "Funy Frostys" Ice Cream and Popeye appears on signs as a mascot for everything from light bulbs to French magazines to his own drink brand. In 2000, the New York Times called Charles M. Schulz' "Peanuts" characters "one of the most powerful and effective brands in entertainment marketing" and responsible for billions of dollars worth of revenue for companies ranging from Fossil, to Dolly Madison snack cakes to Metropolitan Life insurance.[1]

There are just a few popular characters that do not appear on signs. If you see artist Bill Watterson's beloved Calvin & Hobbes characters on a sign then rest assured you are looking at a fantasy piece. According to a rare interview Watterson gave in 2013, almost no legitimate Calvin and Hobbes merchandise exists outside of book collections, a line of calendars, and a rare educator's textbook produced in 1993.[2] In a 2005 press release by Andrews McMeel Publishing, Watterson explained why he

---

1 Elliot, Stuart, "The Media Business: Advertising; Will 'Peanuts' characters remain effective images, or will they go the way of the Schmoo?" *The New York Times*, Feb. 17, 2000.
2 Rossen, Jake (2013, December). *Mental_floss*, volume 12 (issue 8).

avoided licensing his characters: "Actually, I wasn't against all merchandising when I started the strip, but each product I considered seemed to violate the spirit of the strip, contradict its message, and take me away from the work I loved."

VINTAGE TYPOGRAPHY

Typography was born with Johann Gutenberg's moveable type press in 1439 but it wasn't until the mid-1700s that French typographer Pierre Fournier le Jeune standardized the system of measuring type. This system is now known as the Pica system and still in use today. Marketers realized early that type appearing on signs had to be crisp, clear, and easy to read at a distance. They also learned a consistent font is crucial to brand recognition.

The most common fonts used in signs are san serif fonts. These plain fonts without any extra embellishments make words easy to read and stand out from design and images. This style was pioneered in Latin and Greek inscriptions but they served a practical purpose in print ads and signs in the early 1800s. San serif fonts such were widely employed by the 1860s. However, companies adopted serif fonts as well, perhaps none more successfully than Coca-Cola.

We can thank Frank M. Robinson, bookkeeper to Coca-Cola inventor John Pemberton, for incorporated the curvaceous Spencerian script as Coca-Cola's logo, likely between 1885 and 1887. The font was taken directly from the most popular formal handwriting style in use in America from about 1840 to 1925. Many brands that embraced advertising also used this font style on their signs. Ford Motor Company, Cascarets laxatives, Canadian Club, and Campbell's Soups all used Spencerian script – or a very close variation – for their advertising signs. Coke's consistent use of font to brand its product is still replicated today.

A little knowledge of fonts can actually help you date some signs. Helvetica, currently the most commonly used font for advertising, was developed in 1956-1957 by Max Miedinger. It is popular because its dimensions make it easy to read in smaller sizes.

Graphic designers worked diligently to match the right topography to illustrate the variety of slogans created for products.

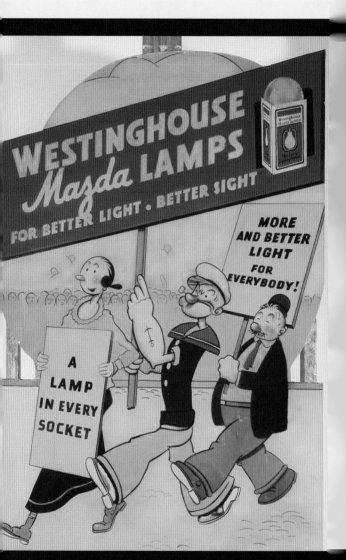

Popeye, Olive Oyl, and Wimpy are the centerpieces of this brilliant die-cut Westinghouse Mazda Lamp sign from 1934 by the Westinghouse Lamp Co. Printed on cardboard, the colorful display capitalizes on 1928 Republican campaign economic slogan, "A Chicken in Every Pot," good with slight restoration, 20-3/4" x 31", **$276**.

Heritage Auctions

AMERICA'S (COMMERCIAL) ART

The high demand for advertising signs, which launched the modern era of advertising, has also been recognized as one of the greatest opportunities for American painters and illustrators. The demand for original art launched the careers of many of the country's respected artists ... only after they designed advertisements. Some of these artists are just now seeing their works emerge on the market, sparking an entirely new hobby of collecting illustration art. The field of iconography is filled with examples of artists whose unsung work helped influence culture and fine art. Unfortunately, the names of many commercial artists have been lost to history.

Following World War II the successful G.I. Bill funded tuition at institutions and universities and The Chicago Academy of Fine Arts and the American Academy of Art, also in Chicago, were popular destination for art students. Thanks to its cartooning and illustration courses, the list of artists who studied here is literally a who's who of 20th century pop culture: Walt Disney, Theodore Lukits, Arnold Friberg, and Haddon Hubbard "Sunny" Sundblom.

Sundblom is best known for painting the modern, heart-warming visage of Santa Claus for Coca-Cola ads. According to "20th Century Advertising," Sundblom's Santa was a cross between the "jolly old elf" in Clement Clarke Moore's "'Twas the Night Before Christmas" and a retired salesman named Lou Prentice. Santa was Sundblom's main focus for 33 years and generations later his art still influences how the public envisions the character.

"From 1915 to 1930, Coca-Cola secured top artists of the day to create their ads, like Haddon Sundblom, who was best known for his Santa Claus Coke ads, and the famous pin-up artist Gil Elvgren," said Dan Morphy, President of Morphy Auctions. "There was a lot of competition in the soft drink market between World War I and II, so Coca-Cola stepped up its game and hired the very best artists to make their ads stand out."

In addition to producing ads for Ford, Lincoln, Packard, Cream of Wheat, and Aunt Jemima, Sundblom also developed Coke's Sprite Boy mascot used on signs during the 1940s-1950s. He doesn't get enough credit, however, for modernizing the appearance of the Quaker Oats Man, whose updated look was modeled after his assistant, Harold W. McCauley.

Lime-Crush Cardboard sign, 1920s-30s, artwork
by Norman Rockwell, very good, 12" x 9", **$5,700**.

Morphy Auctions

Advertising signs also sparked the fledgling career of an
artist whose work recently sold for more than $46 million. The
original paintings of Norman Rockwell, best known for his
painted covers of *Saturday Evening Post*, set a record in 2013,
but a cardboard Lime-Crush advertising sign from the 1920s-
30s featuring his artwork now brings $5,000 at auction.

When all of these elements – the talent, the typography, the
characters, the slogans, and the calls to action – come together,
it's easy to see why advertising signs stir such strong passion
among collectors. As we'll see, that passion often translates into
big dollars. At auction, antiques shows, and at collector events,
sometimes the only thing standing in the way between a collector and a rare find is cold hard cash.

CHARACTER CASE STUDY

Although some trademark characters fade away, others are consistently revamped for changing tastes. A few characters stand the test of time.

Drink Vernor's Ginger Ale double-sided die-cut flange tin sign, 18" x 21", **$300**.

VERNOR'S GINGER ALE "WOODY" THE GNOME

Vernor's Ginger Ale is considered the oldest surviving ginger ale brand in the United States. Popular legend has it that the soda was created, or rather discovered, after Detroit pharmacist James Vernor returned home after serving in the 4th Michigan Cavalry during the U.S. Civil War for four years. He stored a syrup concoction of 19 different ingredients in an oak cask, which to his delight had developed into an unusual drink. The drink was actually created after the war to serve as an American competitor to popular Irish ginger ale. First appearing in the early 20th century, "Woody"

The updated Woody.

the gnome mascot was used in signs for Vernor's until 1987. The character was given an update and reintroduced about 25 years later on soda cases and cans and grocery displays with a new slogan: "A Michigan Original Since 1866." Not surprisingly, Woody boosts the value of vintage Vernor's signs at auction. A Vernor's Ginger Ale self-framed embossed tin sign showing

Woody, in excellent to near-mint condition and measuring 54-1/2 inches high x 18 inches wide can bring more than $1,000 at auction. Plain Vernor's signs without Woody sell for about $100.

Tin Buster Brown Shoes sign, made for Whitwell Bros., nice image of Buster Brown and Tige, excellent, 20" x 14-1/2", **$350**.

Morphy Auctions

BUSTER BROWN SHOES BUSTER BROWN

Buster Brown Hosiery and Shoes began using a comic strip character named Buster and his dog, Tige, in the early 1900s. By 1930, the character was the most widely licensed character until Mickey Mouse claimed the honor in the 1930s. The character was created by Richard F. Outcault, who also created The Yellow Kid. Buster and Tige were licensed to dozens of companies who used the duo to market shoes, bread, handkerchiefs,  and cameras, and a large line of children's books. This diversity means Buster Brown signs from the 1950s-1960s can be found for as little as $100. The most common sign to come to auction is a bread advertising sign for Golden Sheaf Bakery measuring 19-1/2" x 27-1/2" on its own or 25" x 33" framed. These sell for roughly $1,500. A large, Buster Brown neon sign by Kirn Signs measuring 54' x 54" x 6-1/2" sold for $6,555 at a 2006 auction. The logo was recently modernized and is still used today by the Brown Shoe Co., of Clayton, Mo.

This Coca-Cola embossed tin sign, 1920s-30s, is an example of the brand's Spencerian script logo, made by Dasco, very good to excellent, 17-3/4" x 5-3/4", **$240**.

Morphy Auctions

The double Cs in the logo of the C.C.M. company look like they could cut ice in this 1940s advertising sign, which stands as a good example of how advertisers used typography to reach consumers; heavy cardboard, rare, 19-1/2" x 22-1/2", **$717**.

Heritage Auctions

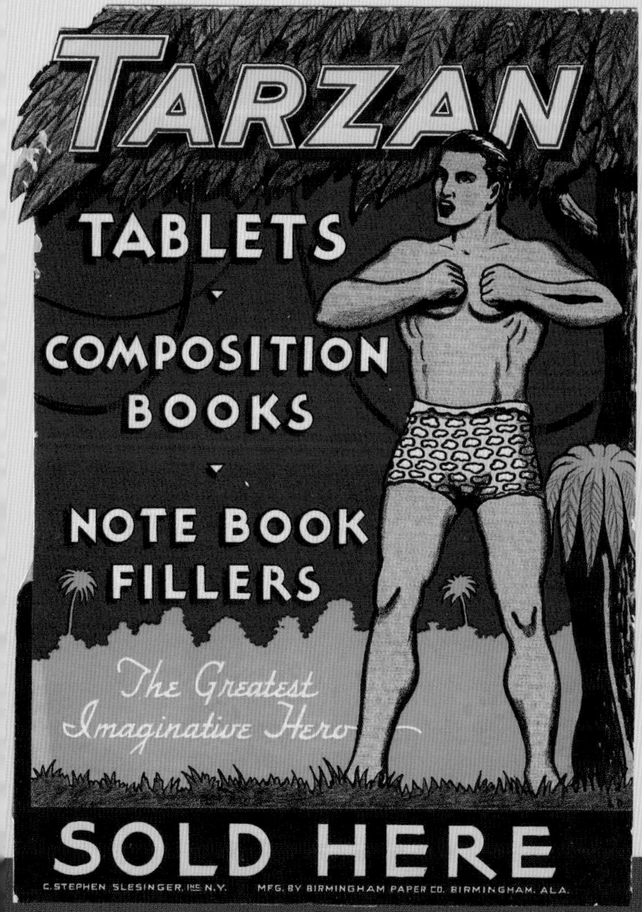

Tarzan school paper supplies cardboard store sign, circa 1930s, Birmingham Paper Co., very good, **$167**.

Heritage Auctions

Comic strip characters were routinely licensed to sell products in the early 20th century. These two cardboard signs feature Physically Powerful Katrinka and The Skipper, cartoon characters from the 1934 "Toonerville Trolley" comic strip drawn by Fontaine Fox, a Louisville artist. Copyright 1934 by Fontaine Fox. The two signs below are cartoon characters from the comic strip "Mutt and Jeff" drawn by cartoonist H.C. ("Bud") Fisher, Copyright 1934 by H.C. Fisher. All four measure approximately 23-1/2" h x 8-1/2" w and remain in very good to excellent; all retain original brass hanging grommets. They sold as a set for **$1,185.**

James D. Julia, Inc.

Heavy paper advertising sign employs Batman to promote All Star
Dairies, excellent, 24" x 44", **$263**.

A long forgotten artist created this original illustration art for
an Anheuser Busch advertisement campaign. "They All Want
Budweiser...Nothing Else," oil on canvas, 13-1/2" x 33", **$2,250**.

Kleenex double-sided sign, circa 1940s, painted in cream, red, and
blue on wood, by International Cellucotton Products Co. featuring
Marge Buell's Little Lulu, very fine, 15-3/4" x 15-3/4", **$92**.

Buster Brown Dealer sign, 1950s to 1960s, paper on masonite, very good, **$30**.

Morphy Auctions

Not all characters appearing on signs were imaginary. Colonel Harland Sanders used his persona as a Southern gentleman to create his Kentucky Fried Chicken restaurant chain. This double-sided weathervane of lithographed steel with original directionals is from the 1960s and was at one time common on top of KFC restaurants in the U.S., good condition, 61-1/2" x 23" x 2" assembled, **$1,050**.

Heritage Auctions

See the little fellow on the box of sugar? The National Sugar Refining Company, better known as Jack Frost, used its namesake to create the character "Jack Frost" on advertisements from the 1920s through the 1970s. This 21" x 30" advertising sign is on heavy stock material and in excellent condition. It is commonly reproduced on metal, **$358**.

Heritage Auctions

CHAPTER 3

The World's Best Signs

In 2013, a Beacon Security Gasoline "A Caminol Product" Lighthouse die-cut sign (shown at left), measuring 48" x 30", came to auction for the first time ever.

"I had never sold a Beacon sign at auction, that's how rare this piece was, so it didn't surprise me when it brought that much," said Dan Matthews of Matthews Auctions, at the time. "Arms were shooting up everywhere. It was a real bidding war." Rated 9.5 out of 10 for condition, or about as close to Mint as one can get, the sign is likely the finest example known to exist. The rare example sold for $55,000 and set a record as one of the most valuable gasoline signs ever sold at auction. But it did more than just that: The Beacon Security Gasoline sign elevated the price ceiling for the entire petroliana porcelain sign market.

The Beacon Gas sign could be the poster child of the sign hobby during the last five years. The modern collector's market has been influenced by a few important developments that still hold sway over prices, demand, and rarity.

REDEFINING RARE

Perhaps the most significant influence on prices and the definition of rarity among advertising signs was the development of online auctions. Prior to the online auction marketplace, the chief methods of building an advertising sign collection was attending auctions or antiques shows, working with other collectors through advertisements, during conventions, or through mail order catalogs. With the exception of auctions, prices were set and then negotiated.

The internet and the development of online auctions changed how collectors bought and sold and radically impacted how dealers could set their prices for average or middle market signs. For instance, a sign for Moxie soda that was once deemed rare by dealers and reference guides suddenly appeared by the thousands online. Besides obvious variants, the chief distinction separating so many choices was condition and the amount of cash standing between two collectors and their target.

SIGN SPENDING IS UP, UP, UP

If recent records are any indication, the amount of cash flooding into the sign hobby during the last 10 years shows no signs of slowing down. Larger economic indicators would tell you this shouldn't be the case. The economic crash of 2008 created an economy with low interest rates, a bond market barely keeping up with inflation, and a stock market that is only now starting to show decent returns. But it's precisely these poor returns and uncertainty that encourages collectors to pursue the best signs as both a trophy and a store of value.

The thought is that if the stock market isn't going to pay up, then one-of-a-kind signs stand a chance to increase in value if you're willing to hold them for a long time. This point was driven home in a study released in early 2014 by real estate consultancy Knight Frank. The firm stated that although art can decline in value over a 12-month period, the return increases 2 percent in five years and "skyrockets to 193 percent in a decade." That rivals the general returns seen by coins, stamps, and luxury cars.

Although the study focuses on fine art, I propose that the rarest signs are seen in the same light by pickers, collectors, dealers, and auctioneers. As you'll see in the next chapters, the very best of the antique advertising sign market carry the exact same hallmarks as Old Masters and Contemporary fine art.

FRESH TO MARKET

If you take a close look at all the most valuable signs sold at auction in the last five years, they all have one thing in common: They are all considered fresh to market.

The idea of great discoveries in the antiques market fuels many a collector's dreams and more than a few cable television reality series. From pickers to pawn shops, everyone active in the hobby wants nothing more than to stumble upon a trove of forgotten signs. The urge to discover a lost artifact is so strong

Campbell Soup embossed tin sign, circa 1900-1901, 39-1/2" x 27-1/2" by the H.D. Beach Co., Coshocton, Ohio, $93,000.

R.W. Oliver Auctions

The sign of Campbell's Soup cans arranged to simulate the American flag remains an icon among early American advertising but the motif sparked a furor about the supposed desecration of the flag. It is estimated that there are no more than six copies of this sign exist because the company immediately recalled and destroyed all of them.

that when a cache is actually discovered, collectors battle checkbook to credit card to lay claim to the discovery. That's what happened in 2011 when a reverse painted glass sign came to market for the first time in its history.

The current world record for the most valuable advertising sign is $165,000 in 2011 for a Rock Island Railroad reverse glass sign measuring 54" x 43". The sign was made in 1890 by an employee of the firm and is believed to be the first sign made for the railway company. It eventually found its way into Rock Island's Los Angeles, Calif., offices for a time before it ended up in a private collection and was passed down through three generations over 85 years. When it came to auction, bidding was fierce and quickly blew its $50,000 pre-auction estimate out of the water.

Similarly, the last decade has seen more important private collections come to market than ever before. The David and Marcia Hirsch collection, the Michael Narvaez collection, and the Jan Miller Bacci collection of Moxie advertising (one of the most comprehensive Moxie collections ever amassed) all enjoyed strong bidder interest. Tampa, Fla., Gotham Cigar Museum's collection of cigar-related advertising in 2011 saw a framed paper La Preferencia Cigar sign sell for $1,770 and a life-sized Indian trade sign by W. Demuth & Co., of New York, measuring 91 inches tall, sell for $38,940. When these private collections finally come to market – sometimes after a generation or more – collectors and pickers respond in few other ways.

CONDITION IS KING

There are too many conditions at play to say for certain just how much a sign's price is influenced when a fresh to market find appears for sale. Dan Morphy, president of Dan Morphy Auctions and founder of the Adamstown Antique Gallery in Denver, Pa., says there are actually four things collectors should keep in mind when evaluating what to pay for a sign: Condition, eye appeal, subject matter, and rarity. Of these four, however, collectors are especially sensitive to one in particular: "People have become more condition sensitive than ever before, across all categories," he said.

So what is defined as a sign in mint condition – a Perfect 10? "To be graded a 10, a sign has to meet and excel in all the standard criteria of subject matter, eye appeal and condition," Morphy said. "A true 10 would be unused 'new-old store stock.' New-old store stock does still turn up. In fact, I bought just such a sign – a Lime-Crush sign that was one of 20 found in an unopened box 15 years ago. It's embossed tin, from the 1940s and in dead-mint condition."

Not surprisingly, Morphy said early signs (1890s-1910) are still holding their value due to scarcity and condition. "The number of older signs that are available, or intact and undiscovered, has not gone up," he said. "For the most part, older signs being discovered nowadays tend to be faded or misused. Signs in nice condition are scarcer, while at the same time, in greater demand. Whenever you put those two factors together, prices are very likely to increase."

This "Best or Nothing" approach to the top tier of collecting has probably been the most influential change in the hobby during the last decade. Values of common signs have fallen and the value of rare signs in top condition skyrocket beyond all expectations. "The best signs bring the best money," says auctioneer Wayne Yoder, owner of W. Yoder Auctions. "The whole category is hot right now but the very best are bringing just amazing prices."

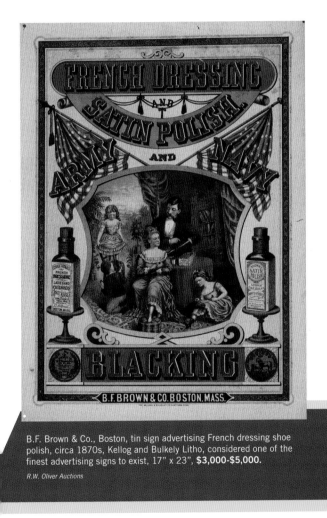

B.F. Brown & Co., Boston, tin sign advertising French dressing shoe polish, circa 1870s, Kellog and Bulkely Litho, considered one of the finest advertising signs to exist, 17" x 23", **$3,000-$5,000.**

R.W. Oliver Auctions

Signs may come in all shapes and sizes, but pickers and collectors all want one thing: top condition. Auction companies say the sign business has never been better.

EXTRA-MINTY!

"Extra-minty" best describes this great Scott-Atwater Outboard Motor sign held by Michael Naylor from Abe's Old Hat Antiques & Country Store of Springfield, Ill. The sign was priced for **$3,500** in 2013.

Brian Maloney

SCOTT·ATWATER

Guide to Grading

In dealing with advertising signs, nothing replaces experience. The following terms and guidelines will help you evaluate a sign's condition.

MINT (M) (10)

No trace of handling. Absolutely factory or workshop new condition. To be found in this condition, a sign would have to have been stored safely from the moment it was made. Sometimes items found in this condition are referred to as New Old Stock.

Coca-Cola triangle porcelain sign, near mint-plus (auction house rating of 9.4 out of possible 10), a brilliant example with strong unfaded color and only miniscule soiling and tiny outer edge nicks; very clean around filigree; strong shine and no surface scratches, 22" x 24", **$16,000.**

Richard Opfer Auctioneering

Golden Guernsey embossed steel sign in mint condition, considered New Old Stock, 17", **$395**.

Brian Maloney

Cardboard Sylvania Flashbulbs advertising sign, 1953, with easel and whimsical graphics, in near mint-plus with no wear, 13-1/2" x 10-3/4", **$60**.

Morphy Auctions

Embossed tin O'Keefe's Beer sign, 1940s-50s, in a homemade frame without glass, in near mint condition with a few shallow bends and crimps with mild stain upper left corner, size framed: 48-1/2" x 19", **$420**.

Morphy Auctions

EXCELLENT (EX) (8)

Appealing presentation and appearance with minor
dents, and scratches, or small chips in enameling or
paint. Paper may show some signs of age.

Self-framed tin Munsingwear sign, great eye appeal, in excellent
condition with some minor wear, 37-3/4" x 25", **$1,320**.

Morphy Auctions

VERY GOOD (VG) (7)

Scratches on the surface, medium paint or enameling chips on edge and minor fading or uneven paint surfaces and may show some signs of rust or pitting.

Large Esso porcelain sign, circa 1950s, in very good condition, with overall smaller and medium chipping with a few bullet holes, 60-1/2" x 91-1/2", **$360**.

Morphy Auctions

GOOD (G) (6)

Scratches or pitting, small dents and small rust spots are common, as well as flaking, stains, fading and uneven colors.

Maritime Milling Co. poultry and dairy feeds sign, in good condition with faded paint, scratches, spotty rust, sold as a lot that brought **$1,303**.

James D. Julia, Inc.

FAIR OR FINE (F) (5)

Signs in this condition are not usually sought after for a collection but they are easy to come by and price is based on availability, eye appeal, and décor value.

UMC Cartridges large advertising Bull's Eye tin sign, 26-1/2" x 18-1/2", tin litho shape of a bull's head with a 1-3/8-inch drilled lip for mounting, American Art Sign Co., Brooklyn, N.Y. In fair condition with extensive damage to finish on each side including nicks and dings along the edges, slight bend to the left horn, **$1,792.**

Heritage Auctions

POOR (P)

Signs in poor condition show extensive damage or wear and are purchased and collected for "industrial décor" due to their well-worn appearance, values are based on circumstance.

Surge Tonganoxie Milking System sign, multiple dents, gouges, bends and extensive rust. Value by circumstance.

Fedora Antiques & Collectibles

The finest known example of a Heddon lure advertising die-cut display sign to ever come to auction is this tri-fold, featuring a leaping bass with a red head shiner scale Zig Wag lure in its mouth, 1930, 26" x 52" h. It opens to reveal a shelf for product, "copyright 1930, James Heddon's Sons and printed by James T. Igoe Co. of Chicago, IL," **$3,000.**

Lang Auction

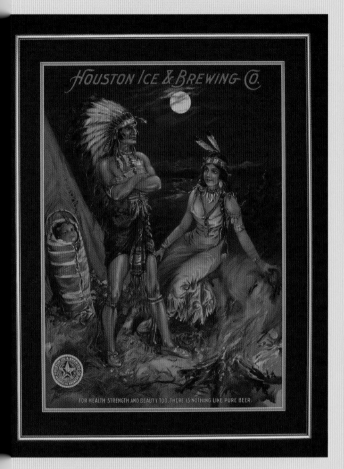

Picturing an Indian Chief, squaw, and papoose, this sign makes a dramatic presence. The bold color and dynamic design of this lithographed paper sign is a fine example of brewer advertising produced at that time. The Houston Ice and Brewing Co., also called the Magnolia Brewery, opened around 1892 and thrived as a brewery business until Prohibition. During their time as a brewery, they produced several signature beers: Magnolia, Richelieu, Hiawatha, Grand Prize, and Southern Select, 16-1/4" x 22-1/2", double matted and nicely framed. Excellent condition as framed, **$3,717**. *Heritage Auctions*

Discovered in the wall of a house being torn down in Maine, this circa 1890 Frostlene cake frosting sign is embossed tin, self framed, lithography from Standard Brands, Coshocton, Ohio, 19-1/2" x 27-1/2", **$1,000-$5,000**.

R.W. Oliver Auctions

De Laval tin sign, green version, in original gesso frame, mint, 19" x 25", **$2,000-$4,000**.

R.W. Oliver Auctions

P. Lorillard Tobacco, circa early 1890s, paper sign, depicting American actress and singer Lillian Russell in five costumes, Giles Litho, New York, framed, rare, 26" x 41", **$4,500-$6,500**.

R.W. Oliver Auctions

Tobacco figure depicting Punch, the Lord of Misrule, circa 1885, retains much original paint, "Wm. Demuth & Co. Manufacturers New York" cast into the base, back is fitted with a metal tube for making puffs of smoke flow through cigar clenched between teeth, rare, 18-1/2" h, **$80,662.**

Heritage Auctions

CHAPTER 4

Trade Signs

It's hard to believe today's pay-per-click and pop-ads can trace their origin to the early days of the Roman Empire. Business owners relied on the most practical method imaginable to advertise their product or service: a large symbol that could be seen and quickly understood by anyone who laid eyes on it. Popularly referred to as "trade signs," the unsophisticated hand-made creations now surpass their four-color counterparts in value by blurring the lines between advertisement and folk art.

Moving beyond antiquity, trade signs flourished during the Middle Ages, a time of high illiteracy rates. The signs changed little for the next three hundred years. Sign making was a healthy business in America during the 1800s. Carved of white pine, the signs were painted, gilded, or polychromed in a variety of colors; there was no limit as to style or type of business advertised. Most were three-dimensional in order to be better seen from the street; however, many trade signs are carved from planks.

Tooth trade sign, circa 1885-1890, American, three-roots, allover crazing, possibly New York or Boston area, rare, **$10,500**.

Urban Remains

Similar to today's businesses, competition was intense to present larger and more elaborate signs with diverse and aesthetically appealing decoration. Themes were used liberally by businesses to help it stand out among the crowd. Animals, boots, whales, watches, teeth, and spectacle frames were commonly used shapes businesses could customize to the taste. Skilled artists decorated the forms with business names and

Trade Sign Key

Scissors = Tailor

Mortar & Pestle = Pharmacist

Hat = Milner

Key = Locksmith

Clock = Jeweler or Clock Shop

Hand = Fortune Teller

Knives or Animal Head = Butcher

Scale = Lawyer

Three Spheres Suspended from a Bar = Pawn Broker

paintings. Few details were overlooked – even the brackets used to attach the signs to the building were crafted by talented metal smiths and are now collected in their own right. Businesses often used signs to show off their talent even though the sign itself did little to reflect the activity inside. For instance, an elaborate zinc peacock might be found hanging outside a tinsmith's shop to reflect the craftsman's steady hand rather than his trade in exotic birds. In England, trade signs were so elaborate that newspapers in the early 1800s pleaded with shops to hang signs that gave customers some clue as to what goes on inside. The April 2, 1710 edition of *The Spectator* newspaper comically explained why the practice was a real problem: "I would enjoin every shop to make use of a sign which bears some affinity to the wares in which it deals. What can be more inconsistent than to see a bawd at the sign of the Angel, or a tailor at the Lion? A cook should not live at the Boot, nor a shoemaker at the Roasted Pig; and yet, for want of this regulation, I have seen a Goat set up before the door of a perfumer, and the French King's Head at a sword-cutter's." [11]

The era is responsible for some of the signs still in use today, such as the barber pole, the mortar and pestle, and pawnbroker balls. But by the 1860s, trade signs were mass produced and fell out of favor by 1900, replaced by more affordable and dynamic advertising methods such as porcelain enamel signs. Fortunately, the diversity of ideas and craftsmanship left collectors plenty to pursue.

1 *Trade Signs And Their Origin*, Cecil A. Meadows.

CIGAR STORE FIGURES

Cigar Store Indians remain the most valuable trade signs among today's collectors. Few other forms of advertising and folk art have captivated collectors and the general public alike than these life-size works of art. The figures stood out front of tobacco shops during the 19th century, especially between 1850 and 1880. Figures are generally 4 feet to 8 feet tall to stand outside shops; however, some were made less than 20 inches high for window displays. The figures are based chiefly on the

American hand-carved cigar store Indian, colorful headdress, bear-claw necklace with central medallion, fringed skirt, holding small bundle of cigars, base: 5-1/2" h, 16" w, 20-1/2" d, headdress to toes 75-1/2", **$203,150**.

Heritage Auctions

Clock trade signs often have hands set at 8:20 to provide the maximum amount of space for the business name and other messages.

This 36" cast iron trade sign for a watch or clock shop sold for **$4,000** at a country auction in Illinois.

Brian Maloney

development of the tobacco trade from America to Europe, which was generally seen as a 'gift' Native Americans bestowed on white settlers.

New York was the center for the figure carving arts and research shows many artists were former figurehead carvers left jobless as the shipping industry declined. Although many shops used figures to increase sales, not all of them were Indians. Several figures, from men, women, and even brand-characters were used in front of shops. However, not all of them were used in front of tobacco shops … and some were not made of wood at all. Zinc and other metals were employed late in the 19th century to create a wider variety of figures, some of which employed mechanical functions such as lighters or puffing smoke. Cigar store figures – whether they hold a fist full of stogies or not – have been mass produced and reproduced for at least 125 years. A quick search for "cigar store wooden Indian" online nets dozens of results and most of them were produced in the last few years. The smart collector will turn to a reliable auction house or a trusted dealer to secure an authentic example.

TRADE SIGN VALUES

Trade signs can be found for as little as $100 to as much as $750,000. Like all signs, size, condition, subject manner, and provenance all influence demand and value. When it comes to trade signs, the more generic the sign the more it is valued in the marketplace. Contrary to other advertising sign categories, trade signs that are not personalized for a business are generally more valuable than one that features shop names or addresses. These "generic" trade signs are eagerly collected by today's professionals who push auction prices to dizzying heights.

In November 2013, a Cigar Store Indian Princess shattered the world record for the most valuable figure of its kind ever offered at auction. The Indian was in a private collection in Louisville, Ky, since 1974 and was sold for $747,500 by Guyette, Schmidt and Deeter in Maryland. The figure was likely carved about 1880 in New York and is attributed to the New York workshop of Samuel Robb or Thomas Brooks, two of the most prolific and collectible figure artists of all time. The two are known for figures imbued with pride and brightly colored clothing. Besides remaining in excellent condition and standing an impressive 83 inches tall, the figure is female – a true rarity among cigar store figures. It is also one of the best documented

An old bicycle is used as a sign for a repair shop in Thompsonville, Connecticut.

Cigar store Indian Princess, circa 1880, cigars bundle in left hand, tobacco leaves in right hand, attributed to New York workshop of Samuel Robb or Thomas Brooks, 83" h, 2013 world record, **$747,000**.

Guyette, Schmidt and Deeter

figures known to exist. Photographs show it standing in front of a Louisville tobacco shop before 1890. She holds bundle of cigars in the left hand, while a handful of tobacco leaves are held in the right.

Trade signs in excellent condition with well-documented provenance – such as the Indian Princess - are the most sought after by collectors, said Eric J. Nordstrom, a trade sign collector and owner of Chicago's Urban Remains Warehouse.

"There's a lot of different trade signs out there. They come in all shapes and sizes made of metal and wood," he said. "I tend to go with the generics. The signs that I really enjoy the most kind of revolve around a subject matter I identify with: optician, apothecary and medical related. One of my favorite pieces by far is a mortar and pestle. Some are illuminated and have glass 'jewels' around them. Collectors will pay quite a bit for those even if they are small."

Nordstrom is working on a book documenting the lost art of the trade sign.

"When you look at old photographs of street scenes, you get a sense at how these signs looked in their original setting," he said. "You can see pictures of mortar and pestles or watchmakers' signs and you see how they were meant to be displayed. I just love it."

Painted pine Astrologer's trade sign, America, early 20th century, in the form of an open book with symbols, 20-1/2" x 23", **$4,740**.

Skinner, Inc.

Boot trade sign, American, 19th century, hand carved, three-dimensional wood with original gilded finish, unidentified artist, 30" h, **$2,000-$4,000**.

Urban Remains

Factoid

It is believed that the three golden spheres composing a pawn broker trade sign are attributed to the Medici family of Florence, Italy. According to legend, a Medici employed by Charlemagne slew a giant using three bags of rocks. The three-ball symbol became the family crest. Since the Medicis were so successful in the financial, banking, and moneylending industries, other families also adopted the symbol.[2]

2 *Trade Signs And Their Origin*, Cecil A. Meadows.

This sign consists of three gilt painted hollow metal balls and a riveted wrought iron wall bracket, VG, wrought iron bracket and metal balls retain most of their paint, 31" h x 24" w, **$1,896**.

James D. Julia, Inc.

Barber Shop
Pole wall mount
illuminating trade
sign with milk
glass "Haircut
Shave 25 Cents"
globe, red crank
turns the pole,
14" w x 42" h,
$1,495.

Victorian Casino Antiques

Steel key sign, old
orange paint, 68", **$472**.

Brunk Auction

Polychrome painted wood and iron "J.P. CAMPBELL'S INN
1844," Vincennes, Orange County, Indiana, circa 1844,
large rectangular mortise and tenon constructed double-
sided sign, 55" l x 32-1/4" w, **$10,073**.

Skinner, Inc.

Apothecary trade sign, circa 1880-1910, druggist mortar, curved etched ruby glass advertising panels on top and bottom in formed metal frame, colorful jeweled center band, excellent with professional restoration on lower advertising panels, rare, 42" h x 25" d, **$12,500**.

Rich Penn Auctions

Wrought iron trade sign,
"El Grifon," circa 1880,
84" h, 68" w, **$2,800**.

Kamelot Auctions

French painted doll store trade sign, late 19th century, one
side painted with a fashionable doll and advertising "Paris
Bebes," the reverse similarly inscribed, with two hanging
eyelets, 16-1/2" x 20-1/4", **$700-$900**.

Skinner, Inc.

Painted and gilt wood trade sign, circa 1900, featuring the Royal Coat of Arms of the United Kingdom and the words "dieu et mon droit," the motto of the British Monarch, unknown maker, possibly London, England, unmarked, 39" x 44", **$5,078**.

Heritage Auctions

Pair of Continental trade signs, circa 1880, probably French, unmarked, 18" x 15" x 15", **$2,151**.

Heritage Auctions

Polychrome
Painted Wooden
"T. DOUGLAS
LADIES &
GENTS QUICK
LUNCH" trade
sign, American,
late 19th century,
tall wooden
panel depicting a
satisfied looking
portly gentleman
with "I Lunch
Here" inscribed
above, 84" h,
26-1/4" w,
$21,330.

Skinner, Inc.

Braumeister cardboard sign, circa 1940s, golf pin-up sign designed to depict sports, drinking, and a beautiful woman, "Braumeister Pilsener" described as "Milwaukee's Choicest Beer," near mint with restoration, 17-1/5" x 22", **$262**.

Heritage Auctions

CHAPTER 5

Beer

The explosion of beer signs during the 19th century can be directly attributed to the competition between regional breweries and the drive for "stomach share" of big Midwest producers. Leading the pack in this genre are, maybe not surprisingly, the same companies that dominate our supermarket shelves 200 years since their inception. Anheuser-Busch, Inc., Miller (now MillerCoors), and Pabst Brewing Co., and D.G. Yuengling & Sons., Inc., may have a smaller market share on today's shelves, but their signs are some of the most valuable and collected on the secondary market.

The diversity of brewing advertising signage is immense and collectors often gravitate to segments that have special meaning. Like any consumable goods at the dawn of the modern

Miller Brewing Co., Milwaukee, 1905, litho on self-framed tin sign, factory scene and Miller High Life girl, litho by H.D. Beach Co., Coshocton, Ohio, very good, 28" h x 39" w, **$4,750**.

Rich Penn Auctions

Harvard Ale, lighted glass and metal sign, 22" dia., **$1,000-$5,000**.
R.W. Oliver Auctions

Oshkosh Brewing Company, porcelain enamel, bottom of the sign is marked "VERIBRITE SIGNS – CHICAGO," active from 1894 to 1971, Oshkosh Brewing Company's chief product was Chief Oshkosh Beer, named for the Menominee Chief who negotiated several treaties and became an alcoholic later in life, base is round convex steel, very good, four grommet holes are arranged 1-3/5 inch in from the rim, 17-1/2" dia., **$3,737**.

Rock Island Auction Co.

Wolf's Beer convex porcelain sign, 18", **$8,300**.

Brian Maloney

Which beer signs will be hot in the future? It's too early to tell, but eye-catching signs from the following companies, or some of their odd brews, may be in demand in the future.

Top 10 U.S. Craft Brewing Companies*

1. Boston Beer Co., Boston, MA
2. Sierra Nevada Brewing Co., Chico, CA
3. New Belgium Brewing Co., Fort Collins, CO
4. Gambrinus, San Antonio, TX
5. Lagunitas Brewing Co., Petaluma, CA
6. Deschutes Brewery, Bend, OR
7. Bell's Brewery, Inc., Galesburg, MI
8. Duvel Moortgat, USA, Kansas City & Cooperstown, MO/NY
9. Brooklyn Brewery, Brooklyn, NY
10. Stone Brewing Co., Escondido, CA

*As of March 31, 2014, based on 2013 beer sales volume

advertising age, brewers quickly adapted the latest technologies to promote their suds. Brewers were among the first companies to truly study how their products were used by consumers. By 1873, the United States had 4,131 breweries, but not all of them embraced advertising as aggressively as others. These regional brewers often used hand-painted signs or catered to taverns on a wholesale basis. U.S. signs are often separated into two eras by a major historic event: Prohibition. U.S. Prohibition, or the legal act of prohibiting the manufacture, storage, transportation, and sale of alcohol and alcoholic beverages, began Jan. 16, 1920 and was repealed in April of 1933.

The Temperance Movement traces its roots to the Colonial period but gained ground the most ground between 1880 and 1890, as some states began passing dry laws with the backing of religious leaders. Industrial or "blue collar" populations opposed the law to the bitter end and as expected the pre-Prohibition signs collected today are often found in or relating to America's grain belt and manufacturing hubs at the turn of the 20th century.

Following the repeal, the number of U.S. breweries initially increased but never hit their 1873 high. Within a year of Prohibition's repeal, 756 breweries were making beer, but the biggest companies remained intent on expansion, using production efficiencies and marketing to squeeze out smaller breweries. In the market for beer following Prohibition, signs played an important role influencing taste and limiting choice. The number of breweries shrunk quickly, to 407 in 1950 and 230 in 1961. By 1983 roughly 80 breweries, run by just 51 independent companies, made beer in America.

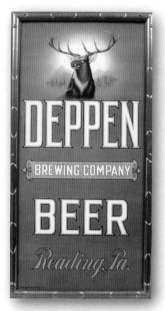

Deppen Beer sign, circa 1930s, Reading, PA., printed glass front with Deppen Stag above Deppen Brewing Company Beer Reading, Pa., signed lower left corner Donaldson Art Sign Co. Cin., O., molded frame with splayed sides and notched-out back for light fixture, sold with original wooden shipping crate, very good, 25-1/4" h x 13-1/4" w x 5" d, **$1,700.**

Conestoga Auction Co.

It's easy to see how the dwindling number of independent brewers (backed up by the push to use cheaper materials in advertising) created two different eras for today's collectors. Kevin Kious, office manager for the Brewery Collectibles Club of America (BCCA) and the author of two books on the breweriana hobby, *St. Louis Brews: 200 Years of Brewing in St. Louis, 1809 – 2009* and *Breweriana: American Beer Collectibles*, said collectors are paying premium prices for pre-Prohibition signs. This is partly due to scarcity, but it is also heavily influenced by the beautiful lithography and artistic talent and the high quality of the materials used in the early advertisements.

"It's almost a whole different crowd that pursues pre-Prohibition signs and those who collect later signs," he said. "There's the issue of expense and finding signs in good condition, but the older signs are like fine art. That's not to say collectors don't pursue the plastic signs of the 1960s and 70s."

This circa 1890s saloon photograph shows how brewery signs, on the wall behind the gentlemen, were originally displayed. Advertising signs from Milwaukee Brewing, Schlitz, Blatz, and Budweiser are on display. The 6" x 4-1/2" photograph sold for **$1,015**.

Heritage Auctions

The fact that most taverns were situated on corners influenced sign design. Many pubs used to be divided into a saloon bar and a public bar. The saloon bar was set up for upscale clientele. Location on a street corner allowed two separate entrances to keep two separate clienteles from interacting inside and out. Additionally, the street corner location made the pub stand out in a block of businesses. To take advantage of this unique location, marketers perfected the corner sign. "The outdoor signs have a certain appeal," Kious said. "There are collectors who also focus strictly on corner signs. If you look at old tavern photographs you can sometimes see two or even three of them. Whatever happened to them all is anybody's guess." Many corner signs are made of vitrolite, a pigmented plate glass most often manufactured by the Meyercord-Carter Company of Vienna, W. V. The company produced glass in black, jade, lavender, and white and images were fused into the glass itself, making it durable and resistant to scratches.

Although glass is a popular medium for corner signs, more examples exist made of porcelain coated steel or painted tin. Most measure 24" x 15-3/4" and some feature the name of the beer, the city or origin, and the brand's chief logo. Some rare corner signs include the name of the bar or tavern itself, and

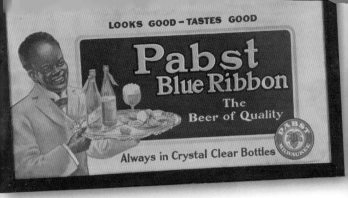

Pabst Blue Ribbon, circa 1940s, cardboard sign, featuring African American waiter, slogan "Looks Good - Tastes Good" and "Always in Crystal Clear Bottles," fine, 20-1/4" x 10-1/4", **$201**.

Heritage Auctions

Consumer's Brewery Company sign, circa 1920s, Consumer's incorporated in 1897, folding in 1930, but reorganized following the end of Prohibition, 14-1/8" dia., sold in lot for **$460**.

Rock Island Auction Co.

Schmidt's City Club Beer, steel with mounting grommets, 54" h x 16" w, sold in a lot for **$460**.

Rock Island Auction Co.

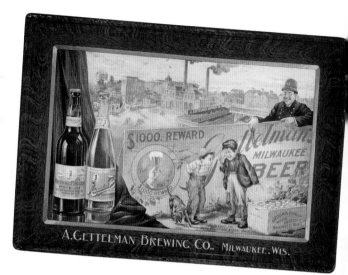

Gettelman Brewing Co., tin sign, self-framed, made by
Meek Litho, Coshocton, Ohio, **$1,000-$5,000**.

R.W. Oliver Auctions

those examples routinely bring five figures at auction. Still,
quality pre-Prohibition beer corner signs can still be found for
$500-$5,000.

Not surprisingly, hobby experts say signs from contemporary craft beer makers are strong candidates for being highly
collectible in the future. "I would say breweriana signs are especially appealing to both younger and older collectors," said Dan
Morphy, President and Owner of Morphy Auctions. "There's
more of a demand overall, so prices go up. These are things to
which younger people can relate."

The future looks bright for beer sign pickers and collectors.
Kious said the hobby is poised to see several major collections
of beer memorabilia, including advertising signs, released to
collectors during the next five to 10 years. "Who knows how
that's going to affect the hobby," he said. "We'd like to get more
blood into the hobby and attract more collectors and joining a
club is a great way to learn about what you want to collect. As
we say, joining the BCCA is like getting 3,500 instant friends."
The group staffs a full-time office, holds annual conventions
across America, and publishes a bi-monthly magazine.

Pilsner Beer, neon sign panel, circa 1940s-50s, excellent, 38" l, **$210**. *Morphy Auctions*

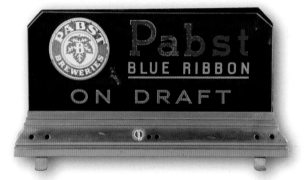

Pabst Blue Ribbon Beer, light-up sign, made by Edgebright, very good, 17-3/4" l, **$780**. *Morphy Auctions*

FAST FACTS: BREWERY HISTORIES

Most collectors focus on signage from the four biggest breweries in American history.

ANHEUSER-BUSCH

Modern men are not the only ones who love the Bud girls; even 100 years ago the St. Louis, Mo., firm used sex appeal to market their product. The first Budweiser girl was introduced in 1883 and she maintained her looks and attire until 1907. This lady sports an Anheuser Busch official emblem on a necklace. The lady's typical pose is with one arm raised holding a bottle

Miller Beer lighted sign, circa 1930s-40s, made by Brunhoff, excellent, 20-1/4" x 16-1/4", **$1,440**. *Morphy Auctions*

of beer. After 1907 the Budweiser girl appeared in a long-sleeve red dress and a new hairstyle. It's strange to think the bikini-clad Budweiser girls we see at every Super Bowl started with blue-eyed beauties seductively showing a tiny fraction of her ankle.

PABST BLUE RIBBON

Founded in 1844, Pabst is one of the oldest brewing companies in America. In 1882 they started tying blue silk ribbons around their "Select" beer. People started asking for that "blue ribbon" beer and in 1895 they officially changed the name to Pabst Blue Ribbon.

MILLER

Miller Brewing Company's most famous trademark is the enigmatic figure known to collectors as the "High Life Girl in the Moon." Miller rolled out High Life in 1903 and at first the oddly-dressed lady held a tray of beer. In 1907 she was placed inside a crescent moon holding a bottle and a full glass of brew, however, signs produced just prior to this show the figure as a circus ringleader of sorts. Around 1944, the figure was modernized and the lovely lady was painted to stare directly at the consumer. It was around this time the company eliminated all other brands to focus on High Life as a result of a grain shortage. The lady figure disappeared from High Life bottles and cans for several years but was reintroduced in 1998. Miller Lite

Schmidt's City Club Beer sign, 30" x 38", **$1,000**.
Brian Maloney

was introduced in 1975, but that's not the first time beer lovers
had tasted that particular recipe. Miller Lite was originally "Ga-
blinger's Diet Beer," developed in 1967 by Blake L. Owades, a
biochemist working for New York's Rheingold Brewery. It found
its way to Miller via the acquisition of the Chicago's Meister
Brau in the late 1960s.

▶ COORS BREWING CO.

Already an apprentice to a brewer in Germany since the
age of 14, Adolph Coors planted the roots for Denver's Coors
Brewing Co. in 1872 as part of a buyout of an existing bottling
company. The next year he partnered with Jacob Schueler to
open "The Golden Brewery." Besides brewing expertise, Coors
had a knack for marketing. Early Schueler & Coors lithography
depicted clear mountain streams, a nod to the quality of the
water used in the beer. The company sold porcelain products
and food products during Prohibition, most famously Coors
Golden Malted Milk. Coors Brewing Company and Miller Brewing Company became MillerCoors in 2007.

It takes some exposure before you can begin to determine the top signs from the average ones. It may be helpful to follow the example set by many food critics: Experience the best and judge everything else against that example. Here are three nice beer signs that could stand alone in any collection, but once they are evaluated side by side, you quickly see why each is good, better, and best.

GOOD

$1,800

This sign dates to the 1890s and has a fantastic image of man drinking a tall glass of Yuengling Lager Beer. It is early and in excellent condition but the frame is a replacement. It measures 24" x 32-1/2".

Photos courtesy Morphy Auctions

BETTER

$5,500

A pre-1900 corner sign in original condition. The fluted metal framework, trim and wooden corner bracket is original and the sign exhibits moderate to extensive flaking primarily to the white background reverse paint. This sign is very rare, but its condition is rated a 7.0-7.5, which is "very good" but a country mile from 'mint.' It measures 16" x 20" x 5".

BEST

$36,500

Yuengling's Beer reverse glass sign made by The John L Dawes Mfg. Co., Pch PA. Convex oval glass. This sign measures 12" x 25" and is in near mint condition overall. It is considered one of the finest breweriana signs ever auctioned.

Kruger Beer, stand-up sign, 3D, near mint, 49-3/4" h, **$240**.

Morphy Auctions

Sterling Brewers sign, circa 1935-40. Founded in 1877, Sterling operated under a number of different names, but produced Super-Bru from 1935-1940, wedge shaped: 2-4/5" w at bottom, 9-3/8" w at top, 17-5/8" l, sold in lot for **$460**.

Rock Island Auction Co.

TRY
GOEBE
It's Mello-ized!

A GREAT NATIONAL BEE
AT WESTERN PRICES

Goebel tin sign, 1951, baseball theme, Detroit-based
"Goebel" beer company, very good, 11" x 14". **$64**.

Heritage Auctions

Cardboard sign, 1952, featuring Sugar Ray Robinson, 2" x 15", **$896**.

Heritage Auctions

CHAPTER 6

Coca-Cola

Far and away, Coca-Cola signs are the most heavily collected advertising signs in the entire hobby. It's easy to see why: the company's dedication to unusually high-quality images paired with the latest marketing mediums solidified the drink as America's brand. The passion collectors bring to Coke's signs is second to none.

Signs from Coca-Cola's earliest days remain among the most valuable. The formula was developed by Atlanta pharmacist John Stith Pemberton in 1886. Like most concoctions sold at the time, Pemberton's drink was marketed as a patent medicine to

Tin sign, 1936, bold graphic with bottle, excellent, 45-1/2" d, **$540**.
Morphy Auctions

cure a variety of ailments. Interestingly enough, although Pemberton created the syrup drink, he played little role in its rise as the most heavily advertised single product in the country. His bookkeeper, Frank M. Robinson, is credited with coming up with the name Coca-Cola around 1887 and the company's second owner – Asa Briggs Candler – is credited with placing the product name on everything from signs to calendars to fans.

The William D'Arcy Advertising Co. in St. Louis assisted Candler's Coca-Cola with its campaigns beginning in 1906. Candler was so impressed with the results, he raised its ad budget from $3,000 initially to $25,000 the following year, or

Coca-Cola embossed tin sign, 1933, good color and appearance, very good, 27-1/4" x 19-1/4", **$1,920**.

Morphy Auctions

a jump from roughly $80,000 to roughly $668,000 in today's dollars. Signs from this period are highly sought after, especially tin signs featuring a straight-sided bottle, which indicate they date before 1915. That's when Coke introduced its familiar "hobbleskirt" bottle. The relationship between D'Arcy and the Coca-Cola brand, however, flowed so deep that the company was retained when the firm was purchased by Earnest Woodruff in 1919. His son, Robert, working with D'Arcy, ensured the marketing machine behind the brand soared.

In the 1920s and 1930s, Robert and D'Arcy set about a plan that fundamentally changed how the brand would appear on signs. Up until that time, Coca-Cola was primarily marketed as a summer beverage; the words "Delicious and Refreshing" were used to promote the drink on the first outdoor advertisement hanging outside Jacobs' Pharmacy in Atlanta in the 1890s. During the 1920s-30s, D'Arcy employee Archie Lee developed a new slogan, "Thirst Knows No Season," and suggested the brand align itself to the most enduring wintertime "brand" of all time: Santa Claus. In 1931, the company hired Fred Mizen to paint Santa on an advertisement and artist Haddon Hubbard "Sunny" Sundblom perfected the figure and in doing so influenced how others would depict the character.

This period marked the "golden years" of Coca-Cola's signs, featuring white Spencerian script against a red ground with

SO YOU WANT TO COLLECT COKE?

"It's always the same: Supply, demand, and condition are so important," said Richard Opfer, owner of Richard Opfer Auctioneering. "Some of the brand new signs are attractive, but if you're looking for signs that will hold and increase, you want signs that are wanted by the most collectors: Go to the 1960s and back. The 1970s-90s items were mass produced. The little trucks, magnets, and Christmas ornaments are fun to own and may be in good condition, but you don't have the rarity aspect."

Opfer advises collectors to inspect the quality of the lithography, be it paper or tin, or standup cardboard. Items featuring celebrities are always desirable, including baseball players, golfers, and other sports figures. "Unusual signs will always be in demand."

Lithographed sign, circa 1904, picturing singer Lillian Nordica, aka the "Yankee Diva" of the American opera scene, metal hanging strips, excellent, 14-1/2" x 19-1/2", **$7,170**.

Heritage Auctions

gold and green borders, now so highly sought after by collectors. Signs of this motif are readily found at auction for $500 to $1,500 or more depending on condition. Between 1928 and 1935, artist Norman Rockwell was hired to create six nostalgic scenes for a line of ads and signs. Rockwell's art blended seamlessly in a wide-ranging yet strategic campaign to depict the soft drink in images essential to the American way of life, a smart decision considering up to 25 percent of Americans were unemployed during the Great Depression.

"Coca-Cola produced the most beautiful advertising right from the start," said Richard Opfer, an auctioneer who's been selling Coca-Cola memorabilia for more than 40 years. "For a 5 cent fountain drink in the turn of the century, it created quality lithography to spread the art it commissioned. It was art. It was truly art."

Opfer said Coca-Cola's devotion to advertising not only ensured the company's success, but it influenced how the world views American culture. With its early adoption of emerging technologies ranging from chromolithography to television and its immense advertising budget ($2.6 billion in 2006 alone according to the latest available data), Coca-Cola's tremendous variety of images, jingles, and slogans solidified the brand as America's product.

"The advertising has been drummed into us," he said. "The advertisements were produced so well and they are everywhere. Who hasn't seen a Coke commercial? And when the ad is made of art, people use it for decorating. These ads are a part of life."

Opfer's company made auction history when he oversaw the sale of The Schmidt Collection of Coca-Cola in 2011-2012. The Frank Schmidt family was one of the first five independent bottlers of Coca-Cola in Louisville in 1901. The successful business was managed through the generations until Frank's grandson, Bill, and his wife, Jan, took over management over and his attention turned to Coca-Cola memorabilia in 1972.

Larry Schmidt, Bill's son, said one of the main reasons his parents started collecting was the addition of a new plant and office building in the early 1970s. Bill thought a few vintage signs and old advertising signs and things would look interesting on the walls and in shelves in the office.

"They went to the Indy Ad Show and bought a number of

things at the very beginning of the interest in Coca-Cola memorabilia," said Larry. "They found fantastic things for reasonable prices. They unloaded it all on the living room floor and began to examine what they purchased that day. They were amazed and blown away at the quality of the lithographs from the turn of the century. The next day they drove all the way back to the show and bought everything they could fit in the car and never looked back.

"They looked at the signage of Coca-Cola and what it had turned into – the geniuses of the advertising."

Clearly, the advertising drove the customer to the product, but at the end of the day, the product has to be what the advertising reflects and it did, Larry said, calling it the perfect synergy of the combination of the two.

The collection held some of the finest Coca-Cola signs known to exist, including a Cameo lithograph paper sign printed about 1896 by the J. Ottmann Litho. Co., N.Y. The 30" x 40" sign hung over a soda fountain bar in a theater in New York City's Time Square. The theater custodian, who thankfully had an appreciation of the piece, saved it in his home, eventually to be discovered decades later by his granddaughter. With provenance from the private collection of Coke scholar Allan Petretti, the sign hammered for $105,000. A monumental 1930s neon building clock and sign, circa 1930s, sold for $50,000.

The Schmidt Collection was on display at the plant and it was moved to a new location in 2005. Bill passed away just two years later, but like most museums, most of the items remained in storage and out of sight. When it was sold, it was considered the largest private collection and brought more than $12 million. Larry Schmidt said the family's two chief concerns were that the signs and memorabilia were reintroduced to the Coke collecting community and that the proceeds would go to a non-profit fund devoted to a better quality of life.

"The auctions really took on a life of their own," Larry said. "The collecting community was very supportive."

Top 10 Signs from the Schmidt Collection of Coca-Cola

1

Cameo paper sign, 1896, produced
by J. Ottmann Litho Co. in New York,
excellent as restored, 30" x 40", **$105,000.**

Photos courtesy Richard Opfer Auctioneering

2

Neon building clock and sign, circa
mid-to-late 1930s, once adorned
the Piqua, Ohio, bottling plant,
the clock face, hands and silver
bezel and trim are metal; the rest
of the sign is embossed porcelain
with extensive neon tubing and
highlights, neon tubing replaced,
excellent, 14' x 7', **$50,000.**

3

Paper on canvas sign, 1905, featuring American Opera star Lillian Nordica, paper on canvas roll down sign canvas is original to this piece, top and bottom edge reinforced with cloth and tacked to wood trim at both ends just the way this sign was produced, framed in Plexiglas box, 25-1/2" x 48", **$50,000**.

4

Tin sign, 1900, featuring Hilda Clark, rare, nail holes in boarder of tin sign, extreme detail in this tin lithography is outstanding, excellent, 20" x 28", **$47,500**.

5

Blinking marquee sign, circa 1930s-40s, in Asheville, N.C., original metal framework, Plexiglas cover, refurbished as excellent, 5' x 18', **$39,000**.

6

Tin sign, embossed, 1898, believed to be one of only two known examples and the better of the two, framed under Plexiglas, rare from the early period in the history of Coca-Cola; highlights the health claims, a 5 cent price, beautiful graphics, early primitive Coca-Cola logo and overall script design of the other lettering, discovered in New England and acquired by the Schmidt Museum in 1989, good, 26-1/4" x 19-1/2", **$26,000**.

7

Tin sign, self framed, 1914, featuring "Betty," all original and untouched, the inside image of Betty inside gold rim is near perfection with outstanding color, gold outline is outstanding, elaborate large outside embossed tin frame also beautiful, near mint, 31" x 41", **$20,000**.

8

Tin embossed sign, featuring Hilda Clark at the desk with early flare glass, elusive early tin sign; lithograph by Sentenne and Green; very good, framed under Plexiglas, 27-1/2" x 19-1/2", **$20,000**.

9

Hanging sign, 1902, celluloid, smaller of the two known to exist, exceptional condition with slight tarnish on gold outside rim, original chain and top adornment, bright green celluloid pops against pure white logo with 5 cent outlined in gold, near mint, 6", **$19,000**.

10

Porcelain double-sided triangle sign, brilliant example with strong unfaded color; only miniscule soiling and tiny outer edge nicks, strong shine and no surface scratches, near mint, 22" x 24", **$16,000**.

Coke Pickup 12 sign,
1956, near mint plus,
54-1/4" x 16", **$14,400**.
Morphy Auctions

Coca-Cola embossed tin
sign, 1933, excellent,
19-1/2" d, **$780**.
Morphy Auctions

Lighted
counter sign,
1930, made
by Brunhoff,
very good,
14" h,
$20,400.
Morphy Auctions

Porcelain double-sided sign, circa 1950s, planned for use outdoor at a service station, original base and brackets, never used and outstanding, **$16,000**. Part of the Schmidt Collection.

Richard Opfer Auctioneering, Inc.

Sonja Henie Coca-Cola advertising sign, circa mid-1930s, one of only two known, heavy lithographed cardboard with added graphic, lettering printed in French, 40" h x 36" w, **$11,500**.

Bertoia Auctions

Coca-Cola cardboard sign, 1940s-50s, excellent, 15" x 12", **$210**.

Morphy Auctions

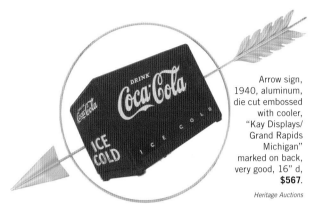

Arrow sign, 1940, aluminum, die cut embossed with cooler, "Kay Displays/ Grand Rapids Michigan" marked on back, very good, 16" d, **$567**.

Heritage Auctions

1931 Embossed Tin Coca-Cola sign, framed under glass a few tiny touched-up fleck nicks, with a small mild edge bend and slight foxing stains on white logo lettering, still displays well, **$3,000**.

Morphy Auctions

Whirligig sign, 1950s, eight panel surfaces, original base mount, near mint, 13" h, **$11,400**.

Morphy Auctions

Coca-Cola cooler sign, 1940s to 1950s, featuring famous Sprite Boy, near mint, 31" l, **$1,200**.

Morphy Auctions

Coca-Cola tin and wood sign, 1948, near mint, 35-1/2" x 17-3/4", **$390**.

Morphy Auctions

Coca-Cola paper football sign, unknown football player, 13-1/2" x 21", **$24**.

Heritage Auctions

Double-sided "Drink Coca Cola" tin drug store sign, excellent, 63" x 42", **$2,000-$3,000**.

Ron Garrett

One collector's travesty is another's craft project. This circa 1970s Coca-Cola sign was crafted into a bench, 60" l, **$795**.

Eric Bradley

Reproductions

Coca-Cola signs and advertising pieces are among the most heavily reproduced. Not all of these reproductions are without value and some contemporary signs are collected simply for their aesthetics. The only way to distinguish reproductions from reissues and fantasy pieces is by experience. Rarely are they marked as reproductions and factories are constantly churning out new fantasy pieces every year. Condition can give you clues to the age of a piece and if you find a sign that seems "too good to be true" then trust your instincts – you're probably correct. Working with experienced dealers and auctioneers is key, but it's always a good idea to secure a second opinion if you're considering making a major purchase – this advice can be from consultants or reference guides, or both. Among the most respected resources include, *Petretti's Coca-Cola Collectibles Price Guide*, 12th Ed., by Allan Petretti, and *The Sparkling Story of Coca-Cola: An Entertaining History including Collectibles, Coke Lore, and Calendar Girls* by Gyvel Young-Witzel and Michael Karl Witzel.

This reissued sign dates to the 1970s-80s. It is in very good to excellent condition, 45-1/2" d, **$270**.

Morphy Auctions

Reproduction red button sign, near mint, 16" d, **$240**.

Morphy Auctions

Fantasy porcelain button sign, near mint, 16" d, **$240**.

Morphy Auctions

This 1989 reproduction is based on a 1935 D'Arcy Advertising Co. sign featuring art by Norman Rockwell. It measures 9-3/4" x 15-1/2" and is often found at flea markets for **$10**.

Eric Bradley

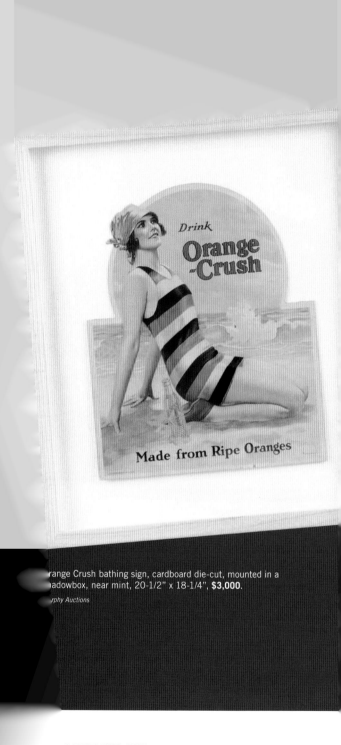

Orange Crush bathing sign, cardboard die-cut, mounted in a shadowbox, near mint, 20-1/2" x 18-1/4", **$3,000**.

Murphy Auctions

CHAPTER 7

Soda Pop

For advertising collectors, the Gay Nineties could be re-named the "Soda Pop Decade." The decade gave us many of the brands we still drink today. It's funny to think that nearly all of the soda brands created back then were first marketed as health tonics when the 21st century considers them the exact opposite. Advertising deserves the credit for building these brands and also plays a role in the demise and consolidation of others. Why didn't Nehi become Coke? What happened to Cheer Up? Who drank the last can of Ramblin' Root Beer?

Generally speaking, most non-Coke soda signs can be easily found at auction for $100 to $400, unless they are in truly exceptional condition. Rare brands in top condition often sell for more than $1,000. These signs are great additions to any collection thanks to their wholesome graphics. They also stand as a testament to an era before corporate consolidation swallowed (no pun intended) a great diversity of beverages thereby limiting choice among consumers.

Here's a trip down memory lane with a few of the most popular soda advertising signs collected today:

PEPSI AKA BRAD'S DRINK

Caleb Davis Bradham invented a soft drink in 1893 that would eventually become the No. 2 seller soda of all time: Pepsi-Cola. Bradham was a North Carolina pharmacist and originally marketed his beverage as "Brad's Drink." Bradham played up the exotic nature of the drink by saying it was made from a blend of "rare oils," Kaola nut and vanilla. He changed the name to Pepsi-Cola in 1898 by combining the words "pepsin" and "cola," claiming it worked as well as pepsin enzyme to aid in digestion – even though the drink did nothing to that

Pepsi-Cola embossed tin sign, circa early 1940s, excellent, 30" x 10", **$390**.

Morphy Auctions

effect. Many food and beverages developed during this time promised similar medicinal benefits as sale tricks but all that changed with the Pure Food and Drug Act of 1906. The drink was rebranded simply as "Pepsi" in 1961. Pepsi never caught on with the public as much as Coca-Cola. The collecting base is smaller for its signs and advertising, too. That doesn't mean Pepsi collectors are not a passionate or deep-pocketed bunch: a Pepsi-Cola syrup dispenser sold for $31,750 in 2005.

Pepsi-Cola President Walter Mack targeted African Americans during the 1940s in company advertisements as well as its sales force – something noticeably different from Coca-Cola's advertising strategy. The company's chief slogan from the 1930s-1950s was "Pepsi-Cola Hits The Spot" as two pudgy police characters named Pepsi and Pete appeared in many ads. Pepsi and Pete now appear on reproduction and fantasy signs. Advertising has always been the weapon of choice between Coke and Pepsi and the two made history battling for "stomach share" in "Cola Wars" that began in the 1980s.

YOU'RE A PEPPER I'M A PEPPER

Dr Pepper's unique flavor has been marketed over the years as a tasty alternative to the two dominate cola-flavored drinks. It was created in 1885 by pharmacist Charles Alderton in Morrison's Old Corner Drug Store, Waco, Texas, but wasn't nationally marketed until 1904. Most early drinks used medical benefits to give the new brands credibility among consumers and "Doctor" Pepper was no different. The first advertisements promoted Dr Pepper as the "King of Beverages," "Free From Caffeine," and pledged to give customers "Vim, Vigor and Vitality." Dr Pepper is different from other brands in that it heavily promoted the "medicinal benefits" of drinking the sugar drink well after it was fashionable. The brand's 10–2–4 logo seen on so many signs from the 1920s and 1930s is based on research that showed the body's metabolism experienced natural drops at roughly 10 a.m., 2 p.m., and 4 p.m. Dr Pepper seized the research in its ad campaigns and developed the slogan for signs and bottle caps that read "Drink a bite to eat at 10, 2 and 4."

The period after "Dr" has been used on and off during the course of the brand's development. It was dropped during the 1950s and the logo was redesigned with a more slanted font but the period has popped up from time to time. The "red brick" logo against a yellow background was used during the 1930s-1940s along with the slogan "Good For Life." The image graced signs, sack racks, street signs, and coolers.

MAKE MINE MOXIE

Moxie originated as a patent medicine called "Moxie Nerve Food," which was created around 1876 in Lowell, Massachusetts, by Dr. Augustin Thompson of Union, Maine. A carbonated version was bottled in 1884. A Moxie museum in Union, Maine, houses a 30-foot-tall wooden Moxie bottle, once used as a soda stand, and other historical Moxie artifacts. This is an annex to the Matthews Museum of Maine Heritage, which is located at the Union Fairgrounds. Every summer, "all things Moxie" are celebrated at the Moxie Festival in Lisbon Falls, Maine. If there's any more proof how influential Moxie advertising was in pop culture, the

Moxie die-cut cardboard sign, circa 1907-1914, fountain display with Moxie's trademark pointing soda fountain jerk, Frank Archer, sitting atop a wood crate of Moxie bottles, American Lithographic Co., N.Y., very good, professional color touch-ups, 20" w x 41" h, **$948**.

James D. Julia, Inc.

neologism "moxie" entered popular American usage by meaning "courage, daring, and energy," as in "This guy's got moxie!" The new word was due almost entirely to extensive advertising.

OTHER BRANDS

The pantheon of soda pop signs available includes many familiar (and even more unfamiliar) graphics, slogans, and characters.

Root beer is one of the earliest forms of soda pop ever created. Hires Root Beer was developed by Charles Hires, a Philadelphia pharmacist, in 1876. It made its retail debut at the 1876 Philadelphia Centennial Exposition and by 1893 it was being bottle and distributed across the nation.

Nesbitt's hit its heyday in the 1940s and 1950s when it was the most popular orange soda on the market. This was thanks, no doubt, to a fetching young Marilyn Monroe featured in its ads. Most Nesbitt's signs, however, feature cartoon oranges, children, or a comical professor. The brand targeted its marketing as a direct competitor of Orange Crush.

Nichol Kola is a child of the Art Deco '30s, as if you couldn't tell by its label. The cola-flavored drink was made by Harry R. Nicholson Sr. in Baltimore in 1938. Its gimmick was a 12-ounce bottle of soda that only cost a nickel. The pitch was pretty successful. It was eventually purchased by Coca-Cola in the early 1950s only to be phased out. In a strange twist of fate, the brand has returned as a premium soda at a cost of about $2 a bottle.

Nichol Kola steel signs, **$180** apiece.

Brian Maloney

Moxie Nerve Food chromolithographed pressed metal
advertising sign, Kaufmann & Strauss Co., New York,
original oak frame, 27-1/2" x 19-1/2", **$2,600**.

Skinner, Inc.

Soda fountain sign, Cheer Up, A Delightful Beverage, manufactured by Stout Sign Co., St. Louis, Mo, litho on embossed metal, fun singing owl graphic, VG/Exc condition, 19-1/4" h x 19" w, **$2,250**.

Rich Penn Auctions

Embossed tin Cleo Cola sign, wood frame without glass, very good, 31-1/4" x 31", **$330**.

Morphy Auctions

Orange Crush cardboard trolley sign, circa 1920s,
excellent, 21" x 11", **$900**.

Morphy Auctions

NuGrape bottle cap sign, SST (single sided tin), excellent color and
shine with minor wear, marked Robertson, copyright 1955,
excellent, 36" dia., **$1,500-$2,400**.

Eric Bradley

Set of soda advertising signs: Botl'O Grape; "Smile" orange soda; "Pop Kola"; Lime Cola embossed tin on cardboard sign by American Artworks; embossed "Royal Crown Cola," good to very good condition; 1941, embossed "Squirt" soda; embossed "Howdy" orange soda; sold as a lot, **$1,303**.

James D. Julia, Inc.

Texaco Sky Chief porcelain sign/pump plate, white outlined T and "Gasoline Super Charged with Petrox" slogan, 22-1/4" x 12", **$1,500.**

W. Yoder Auctions

CHAPTER 8

Oil, Petroliana and Service Stations

Few sign categories have seen such explosive growth in popularity during the last few years as oil, gasoline, and service station signs. Although the category was always popular, HISTORY's *American Pickers* reality television series showed mainstream watchers oil signs could be art. The show follows dealers Mike Wolfe and Frank Fritz as they travel around the Midwest buying or "picking" all manner of collectibles. Auctioneers say the show single handedly lifted the mid- and low-end of the hobby, while drawing greater attention to the best signs that have only recently been brought to market.

What does this mean for collectors? It's a double-edge sword. Greater awareness means signs in poor condition are no longer being discarded. However, prices seem to be rising at both the top end and the low end, making the signs more expensive to collect.

"Advertising is extremely popular now and it seems everybody, even younger people, are finding signs interesting," said Glenn Miller, owner of Miller's Auction Service of Hixon, Wis. "I try to always offer the best signs in my auctions, but even the ones in not-so-great shape are selling pretty well. [*American Pickers*] certainly helped to make the market more invigorated,

Texaco Motor Oil, double-sided porcelain curb sign, "Property of the Texas Company," cast-iron base, "Clean, Clear, Golden," 31" w x 58" h, **$1,495**.

Victorian Casino Antiques

but I also think the lesser quality stuff is selling well because it's not so expensive that it prices most people out of the market."

Miller, who has held specialty advertising auctions since 2007, said gasoline signs remain the most popular among his petroliana clientele, but collectors are also seeking oil, battery, and other service station signs. Among his top lots include a double-sided Chevrolet neon sign measuring 6-1/2 feet long that brought $9,000 in February 2014. "There are guys who collect specific brands and whatever they find interesting. There is still stuff out there," he said. "There're still great signs being found all the time."

THE RISE OF THE AUTOMOBILE

Karl Benz developed the first motor vehicle in 1885, but America didn't see its first vehicle until 1893 thanks to Frank and Charles Duryea. Henry Ford and his wonderful approach to mass production pushed the United States into the automobile era and by 1908 the Model T was changing the face of the country. It's hard to believe that at one time the country had more than 170 automobile manufacturers. The number of companies it took to keep the vehicles fueled up and on the road numbered into the thousands. These included products such as gasoline, oil, tires, brake linings, and lubrication, and services ranging from tune-ups to wheel balancing. All of these and more are advertised on signs.

Coincidentally, the arrival of the gas-powered automobile coincided with the boon in porcelain enamel sign-making technology. The enamel technology (vitreous enamel in the U.K.) brought together sheet metal, metal oxides and glass. The sheet metal was treated physically and chemically to accept the porcelain enamel paint. Holes were drilled to fit custom stands or brackets.

The metal was then covered in a grip coat or background

Whippet and Willys-Knight, double sided, porcelain enamel, 36", **$800**.
Brian Maloney

color made of powdered glass (frit), water and clay and fired in a kiln at roughly 1,700 degrees. Most often the grip coat is a gray color. Once the grip coat was fired on a base coat - generally white - is added in a separate stage.

The addition of different colors to distinguish words, images or logos, was added by dusting the surface with frit, often through stencils. Metal oxides are added to the frit to create a variety of colors. Each color was fired separately in the kiln, sometimes at different temperatures depending on requirements of the oxides. The more intricate the design, the more time and energy it took to meticulously layer color after color onto the base coat. Interestingly, black was often the last color to be added since sign makers generally added dark colors over light colors.

The addition of detailed images or decals required a transfer process that was also fired in a kiln. These images were the last details added before the sign was fired for the last time.

It's easy to see why these signs were used a service stations. No other sign making materials hold their color and stand up to the elements like porcelain enamel. They could be cleaned with a hose, were fire retardant, and practically fade resistant. However, they weren't perfect. Over time it became extremely easy for the porcelain to chip, especially at contact points around holes and grommets. Edges are often chipped as well. And let's not overlook the temptation of a kid with a BB gun or the hunter taking potshots at a porcelain enamel sign just to hear the sound. An alarming number of petroliana signs show bullet holes, although some collectors find them just another charming bit of character.

This rare, 28" x 17" Graham Paige Service tin flange sign, circa 1928, was originally sold to dealers for just $2 from the Graham-Paige Motors Corporation. The company expressly prohibited service stations from reselling the sign to anyone without the corporation's written permission. It sold for **$15,950** in early 2013.

Matthews Auction

THE FUTURE OF PETROLIANA SIGNS

More proof that the petroliana sign hobby is firing in all cylinders is the 2014 acquisition of Matthews Auction by Morphy Auctions. Owner Dan Matthews led a streak of impressive prices realized in recent years, capped by the sale of a rare Beacon Ethyl Gasoline sign (48" x 30") for an impressive $55,000 in an auction that grossed $800,000 (see Chapter 3).

Dan Morphy, president of Morphy Auctions, said the chief reason for expanding into petroliana meant adding an expert to protect its clients from fakes and reproductions. "At Morphy's, a division is only as good as the expert heading it," Morphy said. "Collectors know that if Dan Matthews represents an item as true and original, that's exactly what it is. There are repros in every advertising category, but none more so than automobilia. That's because the subject matter on these signs is very sought after."

Finding a Fake

Authenticating a sign is best left to professionals, but a few thumbnail tips include:

- Rust spots that have not darkened with age
- Enamel chips that expose gleaming steel
- Uneven application of the porcelain
- Missing mounting holes or grommets that appear unused
- Missing or smudged maker's marks
- Authentic signs often (but not always) feature some type of stamp or markings on the back, either a maker's initials or a number to denote the enamel colors used on the front
- Different enamel colors were layered on top of one another, beginning with a white base coat. If you can feel the transition between one color and another then chances are the sign is original

Value Checked For Your Protection, 34-3/4", **$500**.

W. Yoder Auctions

TYPES OF GASOLINE

Different companies offered the same types of gasoline for early automobiles. In the 1920s-30s, cars used low-compression engines and likewise required low octane fuel. In 1921, Thomas Midgley discovered that adding a teaspoon of tetraethyl lead (TEL) to a gallon of gasoline boosted octane by 10 points while also eliminating knocks at low speeds. The Ethyl Gasoline Corporation, a fuel additive company, was started in 1924. Leaded gasoline was the go-to fuel for America until unleaded was introduced in the 1970s and 1980s.

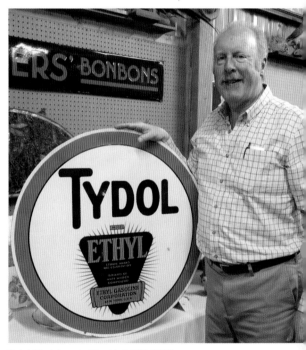

Tydol Ethyl sign, double sided, 30", **$400**.

Brian Maloney

Kanotex Ethyl sign, double-sided porcelain, **$1,850**.

Brian Maloney

Bugatti sign with logo, 12" x 19", **$1,500**.

Matthews Auction

Mobil Diesel single-sided porcelain shield-shaped sign with iconic Pegasus graphic, **$3,300**.

Matthews Auction

Original Mobiloil "D" single-sided rectangular porcelain sign, with Gargoyle logo, **$4,125**.

Matthews Auction

Texaco Lubrication, circa 1930s, porcelain sign, excellent, 38-3/4" x 8-3/4", **$900**.

Morphy Auctions

Pontiac Service sign, circa 1930s to 1940s, good to excellent, 42-1/2" dia., **$3,300**.

Morphy Auctions

Ford (mid-size) oval sign, 23" x 33", **$950**.

Matthews Auction

Richfield gasoline, double sided, steel frame, 58", **$1,700**.

Brian Maloney

Fogg's Drug Store sign, circa 1920s, hand-painted tin, pieces of sheet metal fastened to original wood stretcher frame, "You Au-to Trade At Fogg's Drug Store," Ithaca Sign Works, Ithaca, N.Y.," excellent, tremendous crossover appeal, 73" w x 48" h, **$14,220**.

James D. Julia, Inc.

Frazer Axle Grease, self-framed litho on tin, circa 1900, litho by The American Art Works-Coshocton, Ohio, very good, 25-1/2" h x 38" w, **$1,400**.

Rich Penn Auctions

Oilzum sign, circa 1930s, tin with original wooden framework, has seen a high quality professional restoration, Oilzum graphic imposed over an open convertible with couple, excellent, 61" x 19", **$6,000**.

Morphy Auctions

Standard Oil gasoline, 1940, tin sign, image of Mickey Mouse licensed as part of the most elaborate marketing campaign of Walt Disney's lifetime, lasting 1938-1940, involving an animated short, newspaper supplements, and a line of service station signs, marked Walt Disney Productions, 23-1/5" dia, **$4,000-$5,000**.

Oliver's Auction Gallery

RPM Motor Oil, 1940, tin sign, featuring licensed image of Donald Duck, 23-1/5" dia, **$3,000-$4,000**.

Oliver's Auction Gallery

Hood Tire Dealer
Man, die-cut
sign, single-sided
porcelain, 36" x
12", **$100-$500**.
NOTE: Multiple
variations of this
sign exist.

Ron Garrett

Goodyear Tires, curb
sign, porcelain enamel,
28", **$1,750**.

Brian Maloney

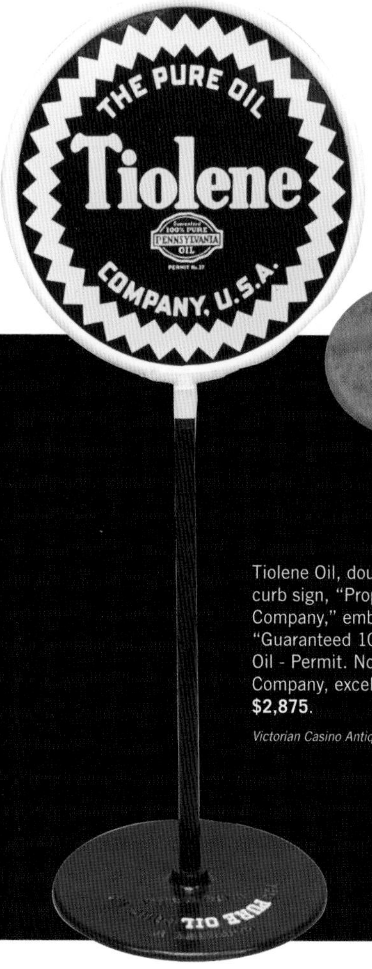

Tiolene Oil, double-sided porcelain
curb sign, "Property of the Pure Oil
Company," embossed cast-iron base,
"Guaranteed 100% Pure Pennsylvania
Oil - Permit. No. 37," The Pure Oil
Company, excellent, 27" x 66" h,
$2,875.

Victorian Casino Antiques

Wincarnis sign, circa 1904, porcelain enamel, "Wincarnis, The World's Greatest Wine Tonic and Nerve Restorative." Wincarnis was a popular British drink that was founded in 1888. A smaller version of this sign was reproduced in the late 1980s. Original condition, 69" x 37", **$8,000+**.

Heritage Auctions

CHAPTER 9

Food and Drink

Most food and drink signs were produced for general or frontier retail establishments dating from the mid-1800s to well into the 1940s. These country stores were a natural evolution of the pioneer trading post as the more affordable source of day-to-day living items, baking and cooking supplies, or goods for general household and home garden use. The development of canned goods in the mid-19th century signaled the need of snappy slogans and mascots. Everyday foods and household items such as rice, sugar, butter, and milk were sold in neighborhood stores from bulk containers until the late 19th century. Companies began to market packaged goods under brand names such as Heinz, Kellogg's, and Carnation. The development of advertising signs for food stuffs marks a significant shift in how these products were consumed. However, the push to market food items paled in comparison to the amount of prints and diecut signs created to market patent medicines. It wasn't until Henry Crowell purchased a mill in Ravenna, Ohio, that someone applied the same principles of marketing to food.

Quaker Oats sign, porcelain, heavily convexed, Asian language characters on each side of the oats container with all other graphics on container in English, heavier surface scratches with edge and corner chipping, very good, rare, 11-3/4" x 23-1/2", **$650**.

Morphy Auctions

Fun Fact

The figure we now know as the Quaker Oats Man was also used on a line of whiskey in the late 1870s. Owner Henry Crowell believed the only thing that would set his oatmeal apart from others was the quality of the packaging and that's where he focused his attention. His trustworthy figure combined with an innovative advertising campaign forever changed how customers made choices about what to buy and why. Advertising scholars often point to Crowell's ideas as the dawn of an age where free will took a profitable turn for companies.

Crowell picked up the working mill after it had been upgraded to process oats that allowed them to be cooked faster than traditional steel-cut oats. The mill also came with a trademark that's still found in cereal aisles today: a friendly gentleman wearing a Quaker hat. The image was registered in 1877, making it the earliest recorded trademark for a cereal and America's longest-standing commercial icon.

This initial explosion of advertising had little to no oversight. Food stuffs, along with soft drink makers, filled signs with claims the product carried medicinal properties – even though none were proven. Signs for Horlick's Malted Milk called the blend of malted barley, wheat flour, and whole milk, "The Diet For Infants, Invalids and Nursing Mothers."

All that changed with the Pure Food and Drug Act of 1906. The federal law mandated product labels "shall embody no statement which shall be false or misleading in any particular." Few people realize this effort took 27 years to become law.

According to auctioneer and antique advertising expert Martin Willis, the ripple effect on manufacturer's advertising claims was significant.

"Coca-Cola no longer mentioned that it 'Cures headaches,' 'Relieves exhaustion' and was a 'Brain tonic' in their advertising. The same was true for many patent medicine companies. Some scrambled to reformulate their products while others didn't – they simply complied with the new law and listed their ingredients on the label. After all, the law didn't forbid patent medicines from containing alcohol or narcotics, it merely said the label has to disclose what's in it. So the odds are pretty good that if the advertising sign you have says that it cures diphtheria, scurvy, malaria, is a swell brain tonic, that it was produced prior to 1907."[1]

1 Fullerton, Phelps. "Collectible Antique Advertisements Podcast & Blog." Antique Auction Forum. 30 July 2010. Web. 15 Jan. 2013.

Froskist Ice Cream double-sided metal flange, product of Electric City Creamery Co., Pennsylvania, 18" x 13-1/2", **$561**.

Bertoia Auctions

Crown Quality Ice Cream embossed tin sign, circa 1930s-40s, unusually framed in Michigan Central Railroad station frame, 20" x 28" (unframed), **$600**.

Ron Garrett

Silverwood's DeLuxe Ice Cream sidewalk sign, 24" x 36", **$225**.

Brian Maloney

Pensupreme Ice Cream porcelain sign, **$1,500**.

Brian Maloney

Embossed "Kayo" chocolate drink by Donaldson Art Sign Co., part of lot that sold for **$1,303**.

James D. Julia, Inc.

Rummy Grapefruit Drink tin on cardboard sign, part of lot that sold for **$1,303**.

James D. Julia, Inc.

Cascarets Candy Cathartic sign, early stone lithography on paper from Morgan Litho Co.-Cleveland, extremely colorful with 10+ colors and famous slogan, "They Work While You Sleep," never before displayed, minor separations at fold line and 1" separation on right outer border, Excellent condition, 28" h x 41-1/2" w, presented in shrink wrap on foam core to protect, **$2,300**.

Rich Penn Auctions

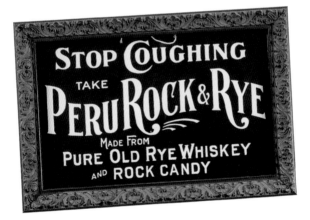

Peru Rock & Rye painted metal sign, professionally framed, 12" x 8", part of lot that sold for **$460**.

Rock Island Auction Co.

Goudey Gum sign, circa 1933, tin litho sign featuring a little sprite whispering in the ear of a young boy, "The Goudey Gum Co. Boston - Chicago," near mint with few light and minor scratches, displayed in yellow metal frame, 7-1/2" x 15-1/2", **$286**.

Heritage Auctions

Dr. White's Medicinal Cures sign, late 1880s, three-paneled paper sign in its original frame, lithographed by the Wm. Burford Litho Co. in Indianapolis, message promotes turn of the century cures for liver disease, coughs, colds and croup, wording is meant to give the appearance of being painted on the glass, but is the poor man's version of that type of advertising, each panel: 9-1/5" x 23-1/4", framed: 36-1/4" x 28", **$1,792**.

Heritage Auctions

EVERYBODY LIKES

Popsicles

A FROZEN DRINK ON A STICK

Embossed Popsicles sign, fair condition,
part of lot that sold for **$1,303**.

James D. Julia, Inc.

Freestone R.H. Cate & Co. Distilleries Knoxville,
Tenn, self-framed tin sign, circa 1905, all original
in excellent condition, 28" x 22", **$3,500**.

Victorian Casino Antiques

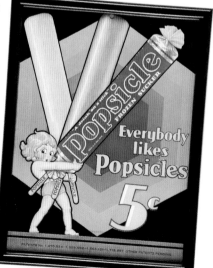

Mickey Mouse promo concession stand sign, 1950s, Walt Disney, animated, Florida State Theatres logo in the lower left corner, good condition with tape on the front and verso, slight paper loss, and crease, 9" x 11", **$69**.

Heritage Auctions

Popsicle cardboard hanging sign, circa 1924, displaying the "single" Popsicle and 5 cent price, framed, 10" x 13", very good condition, sold together with the Abbott and Costello Popsicle sign as seen on page 24, **$191**.

Heritage Auctions

Milkmaid Milk
porcelain sign,
wooden frame,
51", **$1,300**.

Brian Maloney

Grape Nuts die-cut sign featuring Dizzy Dean, circa 1930s,
cardboard with easel back, good eye appeal with scattered
staining and general wear at edges, 40" h x 26" w, **$2,629**.

Heritage Auctions

Moxie "I Like It" die-cut tin litho with girl drinking a glass or Moxie, two small dents near "Moxie," 6" dia, **$590**.

Bertoia Auctions

Paul Jones Whiskey self-framed tin sign, 1903, stunning eye appeal, excellent condition with only random pitting or tiny stain spots about the face of a sign, 28-1/4" x 22-1/4", **$3,600**.

Morphy Auctions

McCormick - Deering Threshers, paper, displays the two varieties of McCormick's thresher line for 1931 as produced for the McCormick Reaper Centennial of 1931, 21" x 31-1/4", **$400-$500**.

Private collection

CHAPTER 10

Farm and Implement

Farm and implement signs are enjoying a resurgence among collectors. Signs priced below $300 are especially popular, but it may surprise collectors to learn these signs often command four figures at auction.

"Feed signs are hot right now," says Ron Garrett, a Texas collector and dealer of signs and advertising displays. "Just about any farm sign, feed signs, implement or anything farm related is in demand these days. The better the sign the more they bring. The sign makers all went out of business, but their signs last forever."

Among feed companies, DeKalb, Arbie, Wayne, Lakko, Tioga (Ti-O-Ga), Lay or Bust, and Allied Mills, all used porcelain signs to promote poultry and livestock feeds. Values for these signs range from $50 to as much as $400 in top condition. I've seen feed signs sell for a pittance at large, well-advertised auctions but sell for more than $300 at country auctions. Interesting graphics command better prices but even straight forward signs with nothing more than text are still attractive. The variety of feed signs is staggering and – as expected – they are often found in the Midwest and in rural communities.

Implement signs were created by the manufacturers but

Oliver Farm Implements "Plowmakers For The World" sign with logo, 14" x 48", **$2,200**.

Matthew's Auction

often ended up in customer's hands. According to a copy of *Farm Implement News* from July 1920, the main benefit of these signs came in reduced expense for the retailer. Manufacturers were the ones who burdened themselves with the trouble and expense of producing their own signs. Retailers could, however, purchase large and attractive signs from wholesalers.

What makes these signs valuable today is scarcity. At the time, farm and implement signs were cheaply made and usually damaged in shipping or cut down to fit odd spaces in storefronts. It's not uncommon to find many a farm sign slashed in half or otherwise "cropped." Retailers would regularly throw free signs in the trash when a new version was sent by the manufacturer. The waste not want not approach to farm

Old Fort Feeds with great graphics, **$1,600**.

Matthew's Auction

life means many tin signs were fished from the trash and used around the farm for patchwork repairs. Still, implement signs were a serious endeavor and marketers encouraged retailers to decorate shops with the best they could find:

"Is there any good logical reason why a progressive dealer, who expects to stay in business, should not decorate his store or warehouse with a neatly lettered but prominent sign that gives his firm name and the line or lines he handles? Such a sign is made to order and fits the building; it adds dignity and prestige to the business, and it draws trade, because it books up the dealer locally with the national advertising of the manufacturer. A new warehouse sign makes people look twice. It proves that there is somebody home."

It's not difficult to see how these ads were perceived as "art" in the late 1800s or early 1900s. Many feature beautifully lithographed prints that romanticized a life of hard work and rural living. The signs of J.I. Case of Racine, Wis., presented highly detailed images of farm machines ranging from threshing machines to tractors as gleaming works of industrial art. The firm manufactured construction equipment and agricultural equipment, opening a veritable sea of signs to collect. The firm's most recognizable mascot is Old Abe, a noble American eagle perched atop a globe of the Earth. The logo was introduced in 1865 and based on a living eagle that served as the mascot for the 8th Wisconsin Volunteer Infantry Regiment. Fun fact: The original "Old Abe" was actually a female.

DE LAVAL — THE WORLD'S STANDARD

Known for producing an indispensable product and beautiful advertising signs, DeLaval Cream Separators are among the most popular farm signs on the market. The company is still a leading producer of dairy and farming machinery since its incorporation in Sweden in 1883. Its centrifugal milk and cream separating machine was patented in 1894 and was marketed to homes and farms across Europe and America. The machines came in different sizes suitable for home or industrial use. The company embraced the latest advertising methods and DeLaval appears on tin signs, porcelain on tin, tin cutouts, and litho on tin die-cut double flanged signs, to name a few. The company's name is presented with a space between De and Laval, although the company's current logo is just one word.

Collectors have paid more than $7,000 for early pieces in exceptional condition. Values for DeLaval signs have gone up during the last 40 years. In the early 1970s, a DeLaval Cream Separator self-framed tin sign from 1906, measuring 25-3/4 inches, was valued at $125. The same sign in similar condition brought $5,250 in 2011. The most sought after DeLaval sign is a tin sign often found in its original gesso frame, measuring 29-

De Laval Cream Separator die-cut double-sided flange sign, litho on metal by American Art Sign Co., Brooklyn, NY, excellent one side and very good on other, 28" h x 18" w, **$7,200**.

Rich Penn Auctions

3/4 inches x 40-2/4 inches overall. These signs feature a central image of a maiden surrounded by four images of various milk cow breeds along with the firm's various separators. They sell at auction from about $1,500 to as much as $4,000. These signs were created with either red, black, or olive green backgrounds (see P. 54).

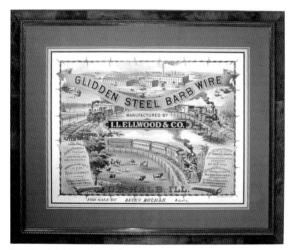

"Glidden Steel Barb Wire," litho on paper sign, manufactured by I.L. Ellwood & Co., DeKalb, IL, Shober & Carqueville-Chicago litho, fabulous late 1800s litho that has been professionally conserved by Kenyon Oppenheimer-Chicago, excellent condition, 28" h x 33" w, **$5,400**.

Rich Penn Auctions

Weighing service porcelain enamel sign, 17-1/2" x 11", part of a set that sold for **$488**.

Rock Island Auction Co.

J.I. Case Threshing Machine tin sign, excellent,
22-1/4" x 16-1/4", **$4,500**.

Morphy Auctions

J.I. Case Threshing Machine Co. tin sign, classic
case company eagle perched atop the globe,
near mint, 32-1/4" x 24-1/4", **$2,700**.

Morphy Auctions

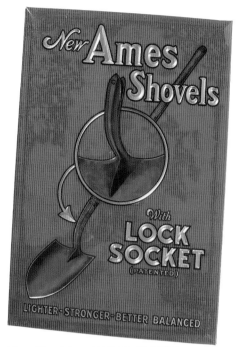

Painted Ames Shovel sign, paper back with folding
stand, illustration highlights shovel lock socket design,
manufactured by Whitehead & Hoag Company, 8-1/2" l x
12-1/2" w, part of lot sold for **$460**.

Rock Island Auction Co.

Case 100th Anniversary sign, painted porcelain enamel sign, 8" l and
8" h, part of lot sold for **$460**.

Rock Island Auction Co.

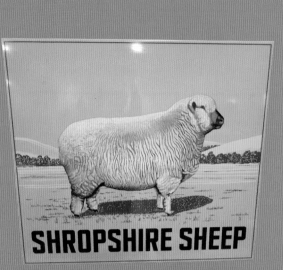

SHROPSHIRE SHEEP

Shropshire Sheep sign, new old stock, original box, 48" x 42", **$1,300**.

Brian Maloney

John Deere
two-legged deer
embossed self-
framed sign, new
old stock, 42" x
38", **$375**.

Matthew's Auction

Funk's
Hybrid corn
seed sign on
tin, 20" x
28", **$125**.

Ron Garrett

Aultman & Taylor Machinery Co. tin sign, single-sided and self-framed, Made by the Meek Company from Coshocton, Ohio, "The threshing rig that leads the world," very good condition, 19-1/4" x 13-1/2", **$2,360**.

W. Yoder Auctions

Pratts Food, the H.D. Beach Co., Coshocton, Ohio, scarce sign that spent much of its life in the same collection as the Lightning Mouse Trap sign shown on P. 12, **$1,500-$2,000**.

Private Collection

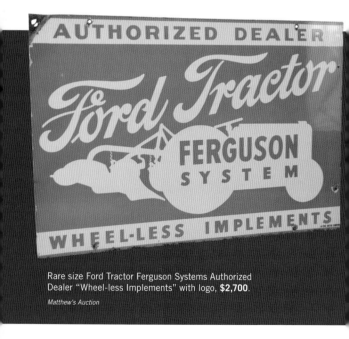

Rare size Ford Tractor Ferguson Systems Authorized Dealer "Wheel-less Implements" with logo, **$2,700**.

Matthew's Auction

Aultman & Taylor paper sign framed under glass, desirable and diverse farm images, rare, **$800-$1,200**.

Private Collection

Rare Swift's Fertilizer flange sign, **$1,250**.

Brian Maloney

Stull Hybrids, easel-style tin sign, 25" h, **$325**.

W. Yoder Auctions

Pioneer Quality Hybrid Corn double-sided sign, die-cut porcelain, 24" x 38", **$1,534**.

W. Yoder Auctions

Warren's Paints, painted and laminated wood sign, "Southern Made for Southern Clime," mounted on iron bracket, several chips, scuffs and minor losses, 48-1/2" x 30", **$350**.

Bunk Auctions

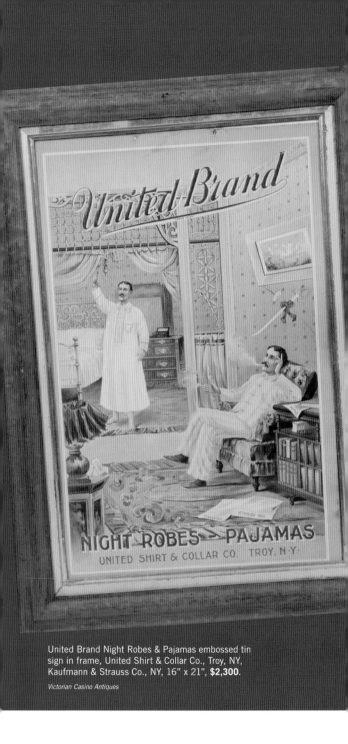

United Brand Night Robes & Pajamas embossed tin sign in frame, United Shirt & Collar Co., Troy, NY, Kaufmann & Strauss Co., NY, 16" x 21", **$2,300.**

Victorian Casino Antiques

CHAPTER 11

Home and Garden

With the arrival of the consumer class, companies used every means possible to reach new customers. Their signs introduced new products and innovations, pulled on our heartstrings, and lent us a chuckle. That is never truer than the signs designed for the most mundane and everyday objects for the house and home. In many cases, the sign's main message was targeted directly at the one person who was responsible for most of the home's purchases: women.

Besides food and drink, American homes were always in high demand of clothing, dishes, soap, shaving cream, and much, much more. From the grocery aisles to our living rooms and kitchens, images became fond memories and slogans turned into household words. Who can forget Burma Shave's roadside signs dotting Route 66 or Alka-Seltzer's "I Can't Believe I Ate The Whole Thing?" Sign collectors hunt for these bits of nostalgia and the results can cause some sky-high demand.

Levi Strauss paper ad with colored illustrations of various overall, koverall and nighties, folds into pair of child's coveralls when removed from frame, 7-3/4" x 32-1/4" wood frame, part of a lot that sold for **$460**.

Rock Island Auction Co.

Cogetama porcelain two-sided die-cut sign, manufactured by Emaillerie Belge, Bruxelles, circa 1936 for the European market, very good condition with a few chips but with surface gloss, 28-1/2" w x 36-1/2" h, **$862**.

Brunk Auctions

TOBACCO SIGNS

Hands down, some of the most beautiful signs ever created were designed by tobacco companies. Cigar store Indians aside (see Chapter 4), tobacco companies were among the first to adopt lithography and porcelain signs. Competition was high to distinguish one cigar from another and companies spared no expense to distinguish their product from others. Among the most desirable signs is a highly detailed chromolithographed sign for Marburg Brothers Tobacco. The company was founded in 1853 in Baltimore and was sold to the American Tobacco Co. in 1891. Rich with symbolism, the circa 1880 print shows two women, one sitting, holding a staff topped with a liberty cap, and the other standing next to a cornucopia. The sign stands as one of the most valuable ever sold at auction. It is just the tip of the stogie of the variety of smoking and tobacco signs available to collect.

Pair of signs: Pennant Cigars Baseball, combination of reverse painting and silver foil inlay and applied paper baseball graphic, "Alphonso Rios & Co., Makers," with holes drilled at top; and Moonstruck Cigars diminutive glass sign, applied paper cigar box label lettering highlighted with foil and mother-of-pearl accents, sight size is 17-1/2" w x 6-1/8" h and 14-3/4" w x 7-3/4" h respectively, very good, sold as a set for **$920**.

Brunk Auctions

Kool Cigarettes NRA sign, circa WWII from the Brown & Williamson Co., good, 17-1/2" w x 11-3/4" h, **$201**.

Brunk Auctions

Seal of North Carolina Smoking Tobacco sign, signed Wells & Hope Co., litho on tin, Phila., PA, rare and gorgeous 10+ color litho in deep walnut frame, c. 1880, Near Mint condition, 32" h x 23-1/2" w, **$25,750**.

Rich Penn Auctions

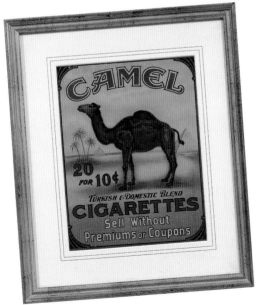

Camel cigarettes transparent door sign featuring a camel, color lithograph on paper, R.J. Reynolds Tobacco Company, Belgian, circa 1915, 9-3/4" x 7-7/8", modern gilt wood frame, **$600**.

Brunk Auctions

Home Run Cigarettes cardboard sign, copyright 1909, stone lithographed advertisement with baseball illustration, by the American Tobacco Company, very good, 11-1/2" w x 17-1/2" h, **$5,750**.

Brunk Auctions

Porcelain Duke's Mixture sign, 1920s-30s, excellent, 8-1/2" x 4-1/4", **$780**.

Morphy Auctions

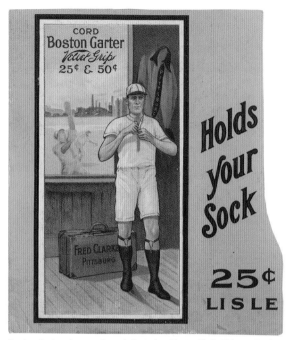

Boston Garter sign, cardboard, featuring Pirates Hall of Famer Fred Clarke, trimmed to 7" w x 9" h, **$5,078**.

Heritage Auctions

The Wizard Shoe corner sign, R.P. Smith & Sons Makers, Chicago, some rust throughout, 15" x 22", **$3,500**.

Victorian Casino Antiques

Expert Hair Cutting porcelain flange sign, **$350**.

Brian Maloney

Winchester Retailer's sign, framed chromolithograph with polychrome applied decal oak, frame labeled "WINCHESTER, Rifles, Shotguns and Ammunition, For Sale Here," the print after H.R. Poore, 32" h, 41-1/2" w, **$3,750**.

Skinner, Inc.

Welcome to A&P! porcelain sign, **$695**.

Brian Maloney

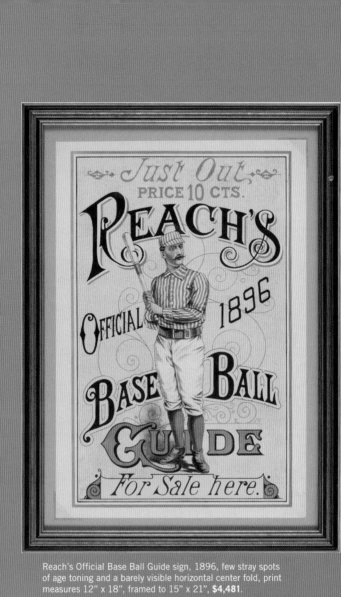

Reach's Official Base Ball Guide sign, 1896, few stray spots of age toning and a barely visible horizontal center fold, print measures 12" x 18", framed to 15" x 21", **$4,481.**

Heritage Auctions

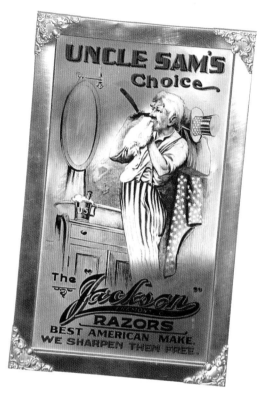

Razor advertising sign, "Uncle Sam's Choice," The "Jackson" Razors, Freemont, Ohio, self-framed litho on metal, outstanding graphics of Uncle Sam shaving, very rare, near mint, 12" h x 7" w, **$3,500**.

Rich Penn Auctions

Rice Seed Co. litho on paper sign, "Rice's Popular Flower Seeds," excellent, 30" h x 20" w, **$1,700**.

Rich Penn Auctions

Skinners Satins tin sign with Indian Chief, early sign, some minor wear on the edge and in the background of sign, minor crimping to curled edge, stellar eye appeal, very good to excellent, 19-1/2" h, **$4,200**.

Morphy Auctions

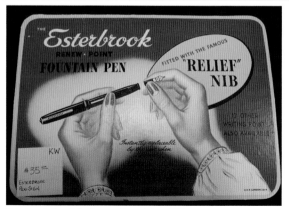

Esterbrook Fountain Pen cardboard sign, **$35**.

Kent Whitley

Stanley with bench plane and curling shaving lithograph point of sale sign, N. Y. Metal Ceiling Co., 9" x 18", **$1,595**.

Brown Tool Auction

New Tariff Range, paper, tying the Taunton Ironworks kitchen stove to politician John Logan, a Senate member until 1886, and strong supporter of protective tariffs that made Massachusetts-made stoves affordable, hence the name "New Tariff" range. It was politically correct late into the turn of the century for a politician to be used in an advertisement. It wasn't until much later that the practice was stopped, making the early pieces portraying political figures very difficult to find and quite rare, 16-1/2" x 19-3/4", **$500-$700**.

Heritage Auctions

Soapine reverse on glass, circa 1890s, some restoration, excellent, 35" x 29", **$6,000**.

Morphy Auctions

Antique Ammunition Cartridge Display Board by United States Cartridge Company, framed under glass in a dark walnut stained reverse bevel frame and gilt liner, featuring 99 examples of cartridges, shot-shells and bullets, below the cartridge display are five mounted cartridge box labels (a sixth one is missing), good condition as configured due to some losses of cartridges but not in major display area, 35" x 40", **$17,925**.

Heritage Auctions

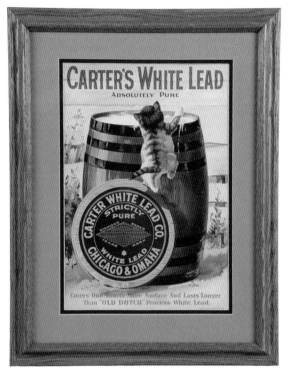

Carter' White Lead paint sign, circa 1895 to 1905, matted and framed under glass, near mint, framed 18-3/4" x 15", **$450**.

Morphy Auctions

The Creek Chub Bait Co. embossed tin sign with the rare turquoise background, **$1,250**.

Brian Maloney

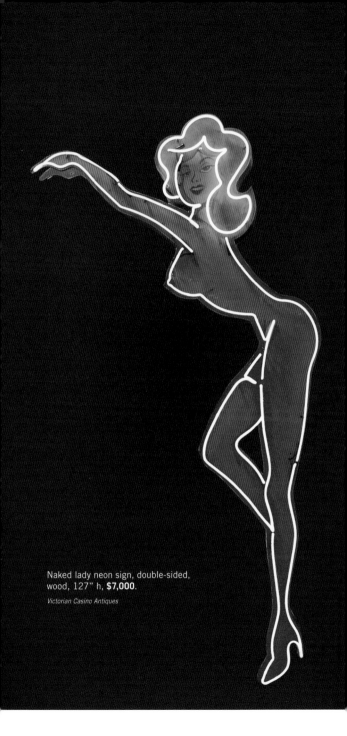

Naked lady neon sign, double-sided,
wood, 127" h, **$7,000**.

Victorian Casino Antiques

CHAPTER 12

Neon Signs

The golden age of neon signs is generally agreed to be 1925 to 1950. Like so many 20th century innovations, neon was developed in Europe and perfected in America. In 1910, Frenchman Georges Claude introduced the world to his interpretation of a Geissler tube, a gas-discharge tube containing rarefied neon or other gases that glowed voltage is applied to electrodes inserted through the glass. The principles behind neon lighting were developed in Germany in 1857. Claude, however, discovered how to manipulate inert gasses to create light while successfully bringing it to market. Considered the "Edison of France," he debuted his "glow discharge" tubes during the Paris Motor Show in 1910. Through a series of innovations and inventions, Claude perfected the development of the gas used in the tubes as well as their behavior when exposed to electricity. He proved that a sign's rainbow of colors, and even some effects, is entirely dependent on the material in the glass tube.

The first neon sign ever made was for a Paris barber shop in 1912, but the first signs available in the United States didn't appear until 1923 – Earle Anthony, the owner of two Los Angeles Packard car dealerships, bought two signs reading "Packard"

Union Made Headlight Overalls, neon, glass, metal, 26" x 14" h, **$1,840**.
Victorian Casino Antiques

for $1,250 apiece. Claude's company, Claude Neon Lights, held a veritable monopoly in the early 1930s and the signs skyrocketed in popularity following the repeal of Prohibition. According to expert Rudi Stern, the signs were a popular medium with the Art Deco movement of the 1930s and came to define the look of the 1950s drive-in diners and the dawn of the Las Vegas strip.

Contemporary interest in neon and other lighted signs is influenced by their visual appeal and the monopolization of Main Street America, said Tod Swormstedt, president and founder of the American Sign Museum in Cincinnati, Ohio. "As branding became stronger, more and more businesses shifted from mom and pop shops to franchises or dealerships," he said. "What you end up with when that happens is a streetscape of familiar businesses. This is true all across the country now. Main Street U.S.A. is a repeat. You see a repeat of the businesses. It shows that corporate branding works but it is at the loss of the mom

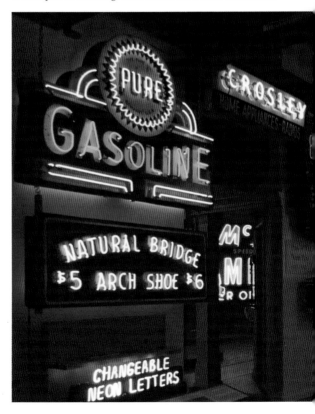

and pop businesses that custom ordered one-of-a-kind signs."

The American Sign Museum is the nation's only repository for signs produced by American entrepreneurs as well as a learning lab for sign makers and those studying sign makers of the past.

Another aspect contributing to demand for these custom lighted signs is the high quality craftsmanship in their construction, which is seen more positively when compared to modern plastic, led-lighted signs. "There's a sense that we have to have things come quickly," Swormsteadt said, referring to modern culture. "Life is fast-paced and these signs, in a broader sense, harken back to a time when things were slower. These signs were not cranked out or mass produced. They inspire a deeper appreciation, similar to how we view the woodworker - it's an old world craftsmanship."

The single technological advancement that hurt neon

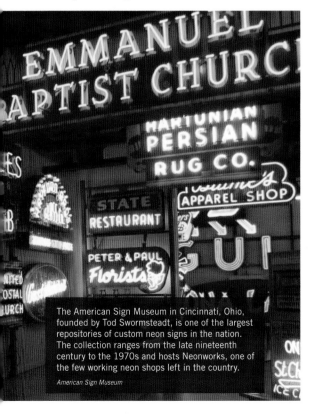

The American Sign Museum in Cincinnati, Ohio, founded by Tod Swormsteadt, is one of the largest repositories of custom neon signs in the nation. The collection ranges from the late nineteenth century to the 1970s and hosts Neonworks, one of the few working neon shops left in the country.

American Sign Museum

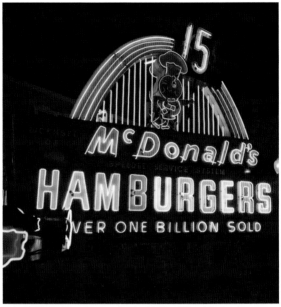

This 1963 single-arch neon sign for McDonald's originates from Huntsville, Ala., and is on permanent display at the American Sign Museum. The sign features the hamburger chain's original mascot, Speedee, who was phased out in favor of Ronald McDonald in the 1960s.

American Sign Museum

More than 500 different neon signs are all displayed on a manufactured streetscape in a town called "Signville," specifically to allow visitors to better understand how the signs were originally displayed.

American Sign Museum

the most was the arrival of the light-emitting diode, or LED, Swormsteadt said. "It took away the need for neon lighting and replaced it with plastic letters. If you go back 15 or 20 years ago, LED lighting took over but neon had been facing challenges before that."

Swormsteadt points to the Highway Beautification Act of 1965 as a fatal blow for outdoor neon. The act called for control of outdoor advertising, including removal of certain types of signs, along the nation's growing Interstate Highway System and the existing federal-aid primary highway system. "There was a huge movement to 'clean up downtowns' and these signs went out of favor, sometimes because the shop owner didn't take care of them. Some places just outlawed neon."

Fast forward 50 years later and it is difficult to find a neon wholesale shop in any American metropolitan area. Those that do exist bend neon for other sign companies. A revival is taking place but only in small pockets nationwide; towns are calling on preservation groups to assist in restoring signs. Cities such as Edmonton, Canada, Saginaw, Mich., and along Denver's Colefax Avenue are all working to replace the signs to draw tourists downtown. "New Mexico spends public tax money to restore the neon signs through Route 66 because they bring in tourists," Swormsteadt said. "It's ironic that it's come full circle."

Like the development of chromolithography, porcelain enamel, and embossed tin, neon's chief goal was to capture people's attention. The development of the neon sign was a significant investment for businesses. This transition period, however, makes it a bit easier to date the neon signs that come to market.

Neon signs are used to promote any number of products and businesses, but primarily soft drinks, automobiles, beer, casinos, and hotels. Even vintage signs are plentiful and are generally found at auction for less than $3,000, with contemporary signs often sold for less than $300. Refurbishing or even completely replacing the glass neon tubes generally does not affect the price of vintage signs, providing the signs' original coloring and aesthetics are preserved. Among the most valuable neon signs ever sold at auction include a one of a kind, Cadillac sign from a Texas dealership, measuring an enormous 32 feet long. The sign, made of ice blue, double-stroke script neon lettering against a white porcelain surface, sold for $100,000.

A reverse on glass Orange Crush neon sign, measuring 18-1/4 inches in diameter, sold for an astounding $29,900 against a $7,000 estimate in 2010.

Whenever there is money to be made, fakes will be found. Some craftsmen take mass-produced signs, drill holes and add neon lights and pass them off as period pieces. Another popular tactic is to split a double-side neon sign, add two wood backs and sell them separately for big money. Working with reputable dealers and auction houses will help you avoid fakes, but nothing is better than inspecting a sign in person to check for telltale signs of meddling.

This GM General Motors Parts neon sign is a good example of how some are adding new neon to porcelain enamel signs. It is 36" and has a new can as well, **$100-$300**.

W. Yoder Auctions

Chevrolet neon sign, double sided, excellent, 6-1/2' l, **$9,000**.

Miller's Auction Service

Super Chevrolet Service neon sign, new neon, new can, painted sign
marked "Walker & Co., Detroit," 50" x 42", **$300**.

W. Yoder Auctions

United Motors Service single-sided neon sign, originally a double-sided porcelain sign, new can, new neon, heavy touch-up from the left "e" in "Service," and in some other spots around the edge, 28" x 48", **$200-$300**.

W. Yoder Auctions

United Motors Service, neon porcelain oval box sign, 24" x 13" h, **$4,000**.

Victorian Casino Antiques

Schlitz On Tap porcelain neon sign, new can and new neon, works, minor touch-up on the "a," the "o," the "n," and up on top, 44" x 30", **$1,500**.

W. Yoder Auctions

White Rose Dealer modified neon sign, new can, new neon, 4' square, **$2,100**.

W. Yoder Auctions

Rexall Drugs, single-sided restored, 72", **$1,800**.

Brian Maloney

Reverse on glass Orange Crush neon light-up sign, working, likely a two-sided sign but only one side remains, rare and felt by many in the hobby to be the most beautiful soda-related lighted sign ever made, 18-1/4" d, **$29,900**.

Morphy Auctions

Duquesne Pilsener light up sign, early with metal display off to side which depicts a man holding up a glass of Pilsener Beer, working, excellent, 24" l, **$720**.

Morphy Auctions

Neon signs are used to promote soft drinks, automobiles, beer, casinos, and hotels. Even vintage signs are plentiful and are generally found at auction for less than $3,000, with contemporary signs often sold for less than $300.

Eric Bradley

Indian Motorcycles sign, neon, contemporary, hanging
double-sided with transformer and housing, very good,
42" l x 11" h x 8" d, **$201**.

James D Julia, Inc.

Coca-Cola Official Drinks neon sign, 1980s, three colors,
two transformers, near mint, 25-1/2" d, **$3,300**.

Morphy Auctions

American's growing demand for signs has sparked a large and diverse market for reproductions. These flea market displays show just a sampling of the fantasy signs produced by the millions for companies spanning farm implements, beer, Coca-Cola and more.

Eric Bradley

CHAPTER 13

How to Value, Flip and Avoid Reproductions

Never before has it been so easy to find an approximate value for signs. You can thank the rise of the internet and generous auctioneers for this development. Most every major auctioneer has opened their sale archives to promote prices realized. It's a great method of publicity and helps collectors and sellers determine fair-market values.. Online auction service providers have also made millions of prices available in exchange for an email address: LiveAuctioneers, iCollector, the-saleroom.com, Invaluable, ProxiBid, and eBay are just a few. Pay to search pricing and appraisal services, such as Worthpoint, have also emerged. Reference books such as the *Antique Trader Antiques & Collectibles Price Guide*, and the one you're holding, put these prices in valuable context.

With all these resources available, what's a collector to do? The answer takes time and patience.

Nearly every database of prices you find at your fingertips is based on auction results. That means each price is unique. The price represents what one individual was prepared to pay at auction for a specific item on a particular date. The fast-paced environment is designed to both sell a large quantity of material quickly and to set a fair market value on the item being sold. But if you've ever bid in an auction, you know how quickly your adrenalin gets pumping, the thrill takes hold and suddenly you've exceeded the amount you originally wanted to pay. That means it's difficult to interpret auction prices as fixed values for any sign.

USING AUCTION VALUES TO APPRAISE SIGNS

The best way to interpret auction results is to compile several comparable examples based on condition, rarity, and collector demand. In other words, instead of starting your search with the intention of finding a single price for your sign ($525) your ultimate goal is to find the range of values at which your sign in similar condition, rarity, and demand, has sold in the past ($400-$600). This approach helps you generate an honest, market-driven value range of your sign.

Here is a good example: Finck's Overalls sign.

Besides being one of the most reproduced images of all time, advertisements for Finck's Overalls feature all there is to love about vintage signs: strong graphics, bold lettering, a catchy tagline. Its famous slogan, "Wear Like A Pigs Nose," adds a dose of provincial charm. But in order to find the value of an authentic Finck's Overalls porcelain sign, you first have to understand the sign's condition, rarity, and collector demand.

Dimensions: Originals measure 17-1/4" x 12"; reproductions measure 12" by 9".

Product history and relevance: William Muir Finck, had nearly 25 years of experience in the men's clothing business (including a stint with Hamilton Carhartt & Co.) before he launched the W.M. Finck & Company in 1902. The firm promoted its union-run Detroit factory as the source of its "Special Brand of Men's Working Clothing," made successful thanks to the booming railroad industry in the Midwest and the mighty Sears & Roebuck Catalog. The brand boomed and Carhartt eventually purchased the W.M. Finck & Co. of Detroit in 1960.

Collector demand: An entire generation grew up with the brand on work clothes and that catchy, albeit comical slogan, "Wear Like A Pig's Nose." A Japanese company is currently reproducing Finck's overalls.

Rarity: Finck embraced advertising and soon used his tagline in newspaper and print ads as well as a large quantity of porcelain signs during the 1930s-1940s. Unfortunately, signs for Finck's Overalls are among the most heavily reproduced signs on the market. The graphics have been reproduced on millions of tin and porcelain signs for at least the last 15 years. This has weakened demand for the authentic signs.

Comparable auction values: During the last five years, signs have sold at auction for prices ranging from $65 to $175. An original Finck's sign in very good condition sold for $960. That means an original Fink's Overalls porcelain advertising sign in average condition is valued at about $100 to $200, with exceptional examples bringing more than 10 times that amount.

Finck's Overalls authentic porcelain sign, very good with small areas of loss around the holes and a few small edge nicks, 17-1/4" x 12", **$960**.

Morphy Auctions

Reproduction sign for Finck's Overalls, 9" l x 12" h, sold in a lot of eight assorted signs that brought **$460**.

Rock Island Auction Co.

Replica metal advertising piece, with authenticated signature by Ted Williams, 10" x 15", **$131**.

Heritage Auctions

REPRODUCTION AND FANTASY SIGNS

Reproduction signs can be found everywhere: flea markets, garage sales, online auctions, and even in antiques shops. Most of the low-value reproductions that exist today were not created to fool shoppers into thinking they were buying the real thing. Most are simply mass produced to meet décor demand, and many are sold at retail outlets ranging from big box retailers to a smaller home décor chains such as Kirkland's or Hobby Lobby.

Repro signs are most often printed on thin tin, but quality porcelain signs exist, too. Some are exact duplicates of existing signs while others are fantasy pieces, incorporating famous products with celebrities or comic characters. Some are licensed collectibles and some are not. Millions of reproduction signs are manufactured in China based on U.S. demand. eBay is repro heaven. Sign makers give four main reasons why their reproduction signs are better than originals: Affordability, Diversity, Size, and Safety – the last of which they claim is based on the lead and enamel paints on original signs as well as a sign's tendency to rust if a chip exposes steel to the air.

The general consensus among sign dealers, collectors, and auctioneers is that reproduction signs have hurt the market. They lead new collectors astray and lower demand for authen-

Repro Resources

It takes a trained eye to spot good reproductions and that's why it's important to learn authentic from the fake. The following companies represent a few of the large-volume merchandisers of reproduction signs. I encourage you to visit these websites often to learn what their inventory looks like. Investing the time educating yourself and training your collector's eye will help you instantly spot a repros and fantasy signs 'in the wild.'

- SignPast.com
- RetroPlanet
- Gas Pump Heaven
- Tin Sign Guru.com
- Ande Rooney
- Garage Art
- Desperate Sign Co.
- Old Time Signs
- OzRep

auctioneers is that reproduction signs have hurt the market. They lead new collectors astray and lower demand for authentic works. "People look at the real stuff and say, 'Wow, look at all the repros,'" says Ron Garrett, a collector and dealer of signs and advertising displays. "When we tell them they're real, they tell us they can buy a repro around the corner for $20. Well, sure you can, but they're not ever going to be worth any more than $20."

Garrett makes an excellent point. As we're seen so far, style, craftsmanship, and rarity make authentic signs an excellent buy that has the potential to keep its value over the long run. Repros have a tendency to trick people into thinking they own the real thing – and that does not help the hobby.

Consider reproduction signs like the art you see for sale at a furniture store or a big box retailer. Does a print of Monet's *Water Lilies* series ruin appreciation and demand for an original hanging in the Metropolitan Museum of Art? I doubt it. If anything, it may spark an appreciation for the real thing and encourage more scholarship on it. That may be true for the very best signs, however, no one will dispute that fact that reproductions do the greatest harm to the value of mid-range signs. The key here is that consumers realize they are buying a reproduction in the first place.

The cold hard truth about reproductions is that they are here to stay. Nearly every auction house in the country has sold a reproduction sign. The respectable ones tell you it's a reproduction in the auction description. But even good, vintage reproductions are in demand. At a large, 2013 Coca-Cola auction, two Asian reproduction porcelain signs sold for $600 and $660 apiece. The auctioneer responsibly noted each as a reproduction in the auction description, but their novelty still appealed to die-hard Coke collectors.

HOW TO FLIP YOUR SIGNS

Selling an authentic sign takes research, patience, and an honest assessment of condition and collector demand. Once the decision has been made to sell, it's time to research the best outlet to reach customers. Here are a few popular ones:

Auctions: A preferred method to sell your best signs. Several U.S. auction houses have staff experienced in bringing great authentic signs to market. These houses also devoted significant resources to promote their auctions around the world, sometimes for months ahead of the sale. The best way to see if your sign is worthy of an advertising-themed auction is to contact the house and send photos of the piece. Be sure to mention all you know about the sign's provenance in your initial contact. It is good practice to reach out to more than one auction house at a time. Ask for their specialist's best estimate on what the auction may sell for and what type of auction your piece may appear.

It's impossible to single out one company, so I encourage you to visit the Resources Section on P. 93 for a list of auction houses specializing in advertising signs.

Shows: Antiques shows are held every weekend across the country. The largest show of its kind is the Indy Antique Advertising Show in Indianapolis, Ind. The show is held in March and September every year and features more than 100 dealers across every advertising medium imaginable, not just signs. Dealers at this show are some of the most experienced and accomplished in the hobby and are generally happy to share what they know.

Flea Markets: A great source to shop and buy but generally

Artificially distressed reproduction fantasy sign for "Klondike-Cough Nuggets," 12-1/5" x 16", found at a flea market for **$10**.

Eric Bradley

not the ideal outlet to sell signs valued at over $300.

Online Auctions: Experienced collectors and dealers search online auction sites and often sign up for email notifications when a new listing's keywords match what they are looking for. Some sellers rely on this attention to make up for their lack of research into an object's value range. This is a double edge sword. It's also difficult for a seller to advertise a single listing on an auction site. The sign's exposure is limited to whoever finds it within the auction period based on how good your description is. For this reason, I don't advise trying to sell high-value signs by yourself on online auction sites unless you've got several years of experience already under your belt.

Glossary

American Art Works Company: Specialty advertising industry started in Coshocton, Ohio in January of 1884, for many years was the nations leading producer of advertising art in the nation, shipping their product worldwide. In the early 1900s Coshocton was second only to New York City in the size of its artist colony. Advertising from Coshocton is on display throughout the country periodically.

Cartridge board: Advertising signs produced for hardware stores and country stores during the 1890s to promote various sizes of ammunition to sportsmen. Highly desirable boards show dozens of bullets, shells, primers, casings, wads, etc. Most commonly advertised brands include Winchester Repeating Arms Co. and The Union Metallic Cartridge Co., or UMC. Boards often measure 54 to 57 inches wide by 37 to 41 inches high.

Advertising: The activity or profession of producing advertisements for commercial products or services.

Celluloid: A class of compounds created from nitrocellulose and camphor, with added dyes and other agents. Generally considered the first thermoplastic, it was first created as Parkesine in 1866[1] and as Xylonite in 1869, before being registered as Celluloid in 1870.

Chromolithography: Developed by Louis Prang and widely used between 1890 and 1920 for printing a colored picture on tin or paper, with each color requiring a separate stone or metal surface. The effect produced both bold and subtle variation of color, the more complex of which are the most desirable by collectors.

Corner sign: A sign made of curved glass or metal designed to hang on the corner of a building or other large stationary object. Some are electrified, but most commonly found made of white Vitrolite glass.

Decalcomania: A decorative technique by which prints or engravings may be permanently transferred to glass. Process was used by the Meyercord-Carter Company of West Virginia to affix advertising images to Vitrolite glass.

Die cut sign: A sign that has been cut into a customized shape by a specialized form tool. Practice was often used in cardboard, paper or tin signs and countertop displays.

Embossed tin: Raised relief stamped or pressed design highlighting graphic elements or lettering.

Enamel sign: Sheet metal coated with a vitreous enamel suitable for holding fast a printed image, design, or words to create a permanent form of advertising poster. Enameling was in use in Germany before English firms adapted the technology in the 1860s for advertising. Entrepreneur Benjamin Baugh opened the first purpose-built enamel sign factory in 1889 and registering it as the Patent Enamel Company. Enamel signs flourished from the 1880s through 1914 but continued until the 1960s. Enamel signs are commonly found measuring 24 x 36 inches.

Fantasy sign: An advertising sign that never existed, except as a new creation playing off authentic designs, slogans or images. Fantasy signs were never intended to trick or fool the collecting public but rather to serve as interesting 'vintage-style' décor at affordable prices.

Gesso: A white paint mixture consisting of a binder mixed with chalk, gypsum, pigment, or any combination of these. It is often used as a preparation for any number of substrates such as wood, canvas and sculpture as a base for paint and other materials that are applied over it and most often employed as to produce ornate frames for advertising signs.

Lithography: Process of printing from a stone or metal plate treated so as to repel ink except where it is required for printing. Process was used on tin, cardboard, paper, and wood.

Logo: A symbol of a company name trademark, abbreviation and designed for easy recognition.

Photolithography: A lithography process introduced after 1900 using light to transfer a photographic image onto a light-sensitive plates. The process allowed the separation into four colors.

Porcelain: Thin, glossy ceramic coating applied to tin and steel which would accept an advertising image.

Provenance: The history of ownership, source, or origin of an advertising sign.

Reproduction: A new sign copied to replicate an original. Most reproductions are sold through wholesale dealers and are often marked as such on the back or along margins. It's when reproductions are sold as authentic, original signs that fraud takes place.

Reverse on glass: A sign composed of an image – usually highly ornate – that has been applied directly to the surface of a pane of glass and then backed and framed in wood.

Schmaltz: Technical term among sign-makers for roadside signs in which the design was made of large (1", 2" or larger) sequins that trembled and caught the light. Such signage was more common before lighted, neon, and retroreflective signs became common. Schmaltz signage almost completely dropped out of use by the late 1970s, but is still occasionally seen, especially to create a nostalgic feel.

Service mark: A trademark used in the United States and several other countries to identify a service rather than a product. A service mark differs from a trademark in that the mark is used on the advertising of the service rather than on the packaging or delivery of the service, since there is generally no "package" to place the mark on, which is the practice for trademarks. The marks REG.U.S PAT.OFF. is common on Coca-Cola outdoor porcelain signs and stands for "Registered with the United States Patent Office."

Self-framed: A sign in which the image and the frame are made of one continuous piece of tin. These signs are often found measuring 18 x 26 inches. Frame detail may simulate wood grain, gilt wood motifs, lettering, applique designs, and mattes.

Trademark: A symbol, word, or words legally registered to represent a company or product.

Vitrolite: A pigmented plate glass used in both flat and corner signs, as well as architectural elements, made by the Meyercord-Carter Company of Vienna, West Virginia, near Parkersburg, in 1908. The company produced glass in black, jade, lavender, and white and images were fused into the glass itself, making it durable and resistant to scratches.

Resources

ADVERTISING SIGN COLLECTING CLUBS

Antique Advertising Association Of America
Pastimes.org
America's No. 1 network of like-minded collectors of all popular and antique advertising. This club is diverse and is dedicated to collecting and preserving all forms and varieties of advertising. It's newsletter, PastTimes, is filled with photos, information, and news about discoveries and research. The club's annual convention is a great place to buy, sell and learn from the experts.

Brewery Collectibles Club of America
bcca.com
This active club publishes a professional, full-color 48-page bimonthly magazine and has more than 1,000 members associated with more than 100 chapters around the world.

Coca-Cola Collectors Club
Cocacolaclub.com
A non-profit organization for all people interested in the history and old and new memorabilia of The Coca-Cola Company.

Petroliana Online Community
OldGas.com
An online community of petroliana collectors, complete with forums, collector advice, restoration techniques, and how to spot unmarked reproductions.

WHERE TO VISIT

American Sign Museum
1330 Monmouth Street
Cincinnati, OH 45225
513-541-6366
info@signmuseum.org
signmuseum.org
Tod Swormstedt, former editor and publisher of *Signs of the Times* magazine, founded the National Signs of the Times Museum in 1999. With the help of a few early believers, the renamed American Sign Museum opened its doors in spring, 2005 with 19,000+ square feet of exhibit space.

AUCTION COMPANIES

Guyette, Schmidt & Deeter
24718 Beverly Rd
St. Michaels, MD 21663
410-745-0485
decoys@guyetteandschmidt.com
guyetteandschmidt.com

Conestoga Auction Co.
768 Graystone Rd
Manheim, PA 17545
717-898-7284
conestogaauction.com

W. Yoder Auction
N 2475 13th Gateway
3 miles W on HWY 21
Wautoma, WI 54982
920-787-5549
wyoderauction.com
Images appearing on behalf
of W. Yoder Auction are
courtesy Heidi Strauss,
photographer

Richard Opfer Auctioneering, Inc.
1919 Greenspring Drive
Timonium, Maryland 21093
410-252-5035
info@opferauction.com
opferauction.com

Kamelot Auctions
4700 Wissahickon Ave.
Philadelphia, PA 19144
215-438-6990
info@kamelotauctions.com
kamelotauctions.com

James D. Julia, Inc.
203 Skowhegan Rd.
Fairfield, ME 04937
800-565-9298
info@jamesdjulia.com
jamesdjulia.com

Victorian Casino Antiques
4520 Arville St #1
Las Vegas, NV 89103
702-382-2466
info2008@vcaauction.com
vcaauction.com

Morphy Auctions
2000 N. Reading Rd.
Denver, PA 17517
717-335-3435
morphy@morphyauctions.com
morphyauctions.com

Rich Penn Auctions
P.O. Box 1355
Waterloo, IA 50704
319-291-6688
info@richpennauctions.com
richpennauctions.com

Adam Partridge Auctioneers & Valuers
Withyfold Drive
Macclesfield Cheshire SK10 2BD United Kingdom
+044 01625 431 788
auctions@adampartridge.co.uk
adampartridge.co.uk

Heritage Auctions
3500 Maple Ave.
Dallas, TX 75219.3941
877-437-4824
Bid@ha.com
ha.com

**Poster Auctions
International, Inc., and
Posters Please, Inc.**
Rennert's Gallery
26 West 17th Street
New York, NY 10011
Tel: (212) 787-4000
info@postersplease.com
http://www.postersplease.
com/

Brunk Auctions
117 Tunnel Road
Asheville, NC 28805
828-254-6846
info@brunkauctions.com
brunkauctions.com

**Skinner Auctioneers &
Appraisers of Objects of
Value**
www.skinnerinc.com
info@skinnerinc.com

Skinner Boston
63 Park Plaza
Boston, MA 02116
617-350-5400

Skinner Marlborough
274 Cedar Hill St.
Marlborough, MA 01752
508-970-3000

Skinner Miami
2332 Galiano St., 2nd Floor
Coral Gables, FL 33134
305-503-4423

**Rock Island Auction
Company**
7819 42nd Street West
Rock Island, IL 61201
800-238-8022
info@rockislandauction.com
rockislandauction.com

R.W. Oliver's Auctions
Richard W. Oliver
207-985-3600
Olivers@RWOlivers.com
rwolivers.com

ONLINE AUCTION
PROVIDERS

- LiveAuctioneers.com
- Proxibid.com
- iCollector.com
- the-saleroom.com

ADVERTISING SHOWS

Indy Antique Advertising Show
March & September
Champions Pavilion at the Indiana State Fairgrounds
1202 E. 38th Street
Indianapolis, IN 42605
217-821-1294
sales@indyadshow.com
indyadshow.com

Chicagoland Antique Advertising,
Slot-Machine & Jukebox Show
April & November
Tilt Promotions, Inc.
P.O. Box 545
Wadsworth, IL 60083
815-353-1593 or 847-244-9263
chicagolandshow.com

DEALERS

Eric J. Nordstrom
urban remains warehouse
1850 W. Grand Ave.
Chicago, IL 60622

urban remains showroom
1818 W. Grand Ave.
Chicago, IL 60622
312-492-6254
urbanremainschicago.com
Bldg. 51 Museum and Artifact Gallery
www.bldg51.com

Darryl Tilden
RoadRelics.com
612-723-1999
roadrelics@aol.com

Ron Garrett
1616 Frost
Gilmer, TX 75644
903-843-5740 or 903-343-8360
Rongarrett13@gmail.com

BIBLIOGRAPHY

Anderton, Mark and Mullen, Sherry. *Gas Station Collectibles.* Radnor, Philadelphia: Wallace-Homestead Book Company, 1994.

Baglee, Christopher and Morley, Andrew. *Enamel Advertising Signs.* Buckinghamshire: Shire Publications, Ltd., 2001.

Congdon-Martin, Douglas. *America For Sale.* West Chester: Schiffer Publishing Co., 1991.

Cope, Jim. *Collectable Old Advertising.* Orange, Texas: 1971.

Hake, Ted. *Hake's Guide to Advertising Collectibles.* Iola: Krause Publications, 1992.

Hake, Ted. *A Treasury of Advertising Collectibles.* New York: Dafran House, 1973.

Huxford, Bob and Sharon. *Huxford's Collectible Advertising*, 3rd Ed. Paducah: Collector Books, 1997.

Last, Jay T. *The Color Explosion: Nineteenth-Century American Lithography.* Santa Ana: Hillcrest Press, 2005.

Lipman, Jean and Winchester, Alice. *The Flowering of American Folk Art.* Philadelphia: Courage Books, 1974.

Meadows, Cecil. *Trade Signs and Their Origin.* London: Routledge & Kegan Paul, 1957.

Pearce, Christopher. *The Catalog of American Collectibles.* New York: Mallard Press, 1990.

Rossen, Jake (2013, December). *Mental_floss*, volume 12 (issue 8). Print.

Saunders, Dave. *Twentieth Century Advertising.* London: Carlton Books Limited, 1999.

Smith, Andrew F. *Eating History: 30 Turning Points in the Making of American Cuisine.* Columbia University Press: New York., 2011.

Williams, R.S. "The Sign of the Farm Equipment Establishment." *Farm Implement News.* Vol. 41 No. 30, July 20,1920: 28-29.

Willis, Martin and Fullerton, Phelps. "Collectible Antique Advertisements Podcast & Blog." Antique Auction Forum. Phelps Fullerton, 30 July 2010. Web. 15 Jan. 2013.

Index

About the Author

Eric Bradley is Heritage Auctions' Public Relations Associate and is editor of the *Antique Trader Antiques & Collectibles Price Guide*, America's No. 1 selling annual collectibles reference book. An award-winning investigative journalist with a degree in Economics, Bradley has written hundreds of articles about antiques and collectibles and has appeared in  *The Wall Street Journal*, *Wired Magazine* and *Four Seasons Magazine* as an expert on the collectibles market. His first book, *Mantiques: A Manly Guide to Cool Stuff*, was published in 2014 and most recently he has been a guest speaker on collectibles as alternative investments.

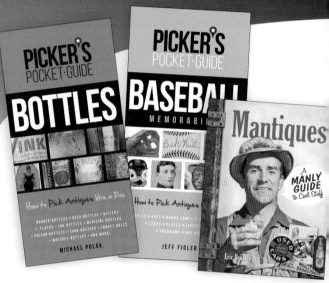